the vital vegan

the vital vegan

MORE THAN 100 VIBRANT PLANT-BASED RECIPES TO ENERGIZE AND NOURISH

LEAH VANDERVELDT

photography by CLARE WINFIELD

RYLAND PETERS & SMALL
LONDON • NEW YORK

Dedication:
For Fabian, Husband of the Year

Senior Designer Megan Smith
Editor Alice Sambrook
Production Manager Gordana
   Simakovic
Editorial Director Julia Charles
Art Director Leslie Harrington
Publisher Cindy Richards

Food Stylist Emily Kydd
Prop Stylist Jennifer Kay

Indexer Vanessa Bird

First published in 2017
as *The New Nourishing*.
This edition published in 2023
by Ryland Peters & Small
20–21 Jockey's Fields
London WC1R 4BW
and
341 E 116th Street
New York, 10029
www.rylandpeters.com

10 9 8 7 6 5 4 3 2 1

ISBN: 978-1-78879-497-8

A CIP record for this book is available
from the British Library.
US Library of Congress CIP data has
been applied for.

Printed in China

Notes
• Both British (Metric) and American
(Imperial plus US cups)
measurements are included in these
recipes for convenience; however it
is important to work with one set
of measurements and not alternate
between the two within a recipe.
• All spoon measurements are level
unless otherwise specified.
• Ovens should be preheated
to the specified temperatures.
We recommend using an oven
thermometer. If using a fan-assisted
oven, adjust temperatures according
to the manufacturer's instructions.
• When a recipe calls for the grated
zest of citrus fruit, buy unwaxed fruit
and wash well before using. If you
can only find treated fruit, scrub well
in warm soapy water before using.
• Always use sterilized jars. For more
information visit the Food Standards
Agency (FSA) website in the UK or
the United States Department of
Agriculture (USDA) website in the US.

Disclaimer
The views expressed in this book are
those of the author, but they are
general views only, and readers are
urged to consult a relevant and
qualified specialist or physician for
individual advice before beginning
any dietary regimen.

contents

Introduction   6

The Basics   8

Breakfasts   24

Soups & Stews   46

Big Bowls   72

Entertaining   102

Savoury Snacks for Sharing   138

Desserts & Sweet Treats   154

Index   174

Acknowledgments   176

introduction

When wondering how to kick this whole thing off, I thought I'd start with the truest thing I know: vegetables are badass. They're tough, beautiful and packed with flavour and nutrients.

Something special happens when you blend good, fresh plant foods with great flavours – you actually begin craving these dishes day after day, not only for how they taste but also for how they make you feel. Plant-based comfort food is all about combining healthful ingredients in ways that make you feel all warm and fuzzy on both a physical and mental level. Using robust flavours, varying textures and being generous with ingredients are some of the key secrets to creating meals that are the perfect combination of satisfying and nourishing.

The concept of the new nourishing is about combining nutritious foods with rich flavours to capture the feelings of indulgence and balance simultaneously. It's a seasonal, vegetable-centric, flexible and flavour-focused way of preparing meals. It makes me feel like I'm taking care of myself in a very tangible way – feeling well-fed and content is what I strive for in life, and this style of cooking is how I get there.

Plant-based comfort is more than warmth, richness and nostalgia (although it can definitely be about those things, too), it's also about fostering a healthy connection to the tastes that you crave and honouring them by making hearty dishes with vegetables, whole foods and herbs and spices at their centre.

Before we start, I'd like to highlight a few things that you will definitely NOT see in this book:

1. Counting calories

I don't count calories. Personally, I don't think it's a sustainable or joyful way to live. I think focusing on eating to feel satisfied and at peace with what's on your plate is far more beneficial.

2. 'Guilt-free food'

Guilt-free implies there should be guilt present in our relationship to food, an ethos which I strongly disagree with. I don't believe in associating 'good' or 'bad' connotations with food. I believe in eating what makes you feel truly good in the moment in a way that you find most enjoyable.

3. Banning foods (or dieting)

While this book focuses mostly on plant-based and vegan cooking, and I encourage use of whole, unprocessed foods the majority of the time, the truth is that all food has a place in our lives. Sure, some foods are more nutrient-dense than others, but I'm careful to say that those are not always the best ones for us.

As with anything, healthy eating can be taken too far. Stressing about eating the 'right' or 'wrong' thing doesn't feel good. I believe if it's causing us stress, it's not doing us much good in the long run anyway. Food is at the heart of our everyday lives and deserves to be fully embraced.

Now that we have the no's out of the way, here are a few things I say a big YES to:

1. Plant-based whole foods

It's pretty clear that vegetables, fruits, legumes, nuts and whole grains are good for our health and sustained well-being. If we can base the majority of our meals around nourishing, nutrient-dense plants, we're likely to reap all kinds of benefits that improve the quality of our lives – like better digestion, more energy and clear headedness.

2. Seasoning and citrus

Seasoning is the key to making vegetables and plant-based foods taste good. If you're cooking your own food from scratch rather than eating processed foods, you can afford to use a little more salt.

I urge you to season to taste throughout this book. If something tastes a little meh, try adding a pinch more salt or a squeeze of fresh lemon juice to it. Chances are, it's one of those two things that can really make a dish shine.

3. Finding your feel-good point

I guess this could also be classified as self-care, but self-care can sound like a vague chore that may or may not involve taking a bath. Instead, I think of Adriene Mishler's Yoga with Adriene's tagline: 'Find What Feels Good', because it's applicable to pretty much everything in life.

Finding your feel-good point is about tuning in to what makes you feel energized, satiated and happy, and doing more of that.

Comfort should be about what makes you feel cared for and peaceful. In the realm of food, this means taking the time to create meals with fresh ingredients that are both substantial and, most importantly, delicious.

My hope for this book is that it inspires you to cook more plant-centric meals in ways that feel good to you. I want to give you the courage to improvise, add to, or subtract from, a recipe to suit your tastes or mood. And to realize that at the end of the day, cooking and eating should be about making you feel your best.

the basics

For mixing, matching and maximizing flavour. These add-ons can take a bowl full of veggies from just okay to crazy-good.

PLANT-EATERS' PROTEIN

crispy chickpeas

The key to extra crunchy and addictive crispy chickpeas is making sure they are as dry as you can get them before you combine them with olive oil and spices. These are great as a snack on their own or as a topper for salads and bowls.

You can mix up the flavour coating with different combinations like madras curry, ras-el-hanout or simple rosemary and thyme.

210 g/1½ cups cooked chickpeas, drained well
1 tablespoon olive oil
1 teaspoon smoked paprika
¼ teaspoon cayenne pepper (optional)
salt, to taste

SERVES 4

Preheat the oven to 200°C (400°F) Gas 6.

Dry the chickpeas on a clean kitchen cloth or paper towels to remove any excess moisture.

In a medium bowl, toss the dry chickpeas with the olive oil, spices and salt to taste. Spread out on a baking tray and bake in the preheated oven for about 25–30 minutes, shaking the tray halfway through, until beginning to brown.

Remove from the oven and allow the chickpeas to cool on the baking tray (they will continue to crisp up more during this time), before serving. Once fully cooled, the chickpeas will keep for 3–4 days in a sealed container in the fridge.

barbecue black beans

I was that picky kid who didn't really like the flavour of ketchup, I had no time for mayo and I still don't totally get what yellow mustard is all about. But I'm a sucker for a good barbecue sauce.

Smoky-sweet and tangy, good barbecue sauce is something to savour. This recipe captures the classic taste with the help of smoked paprika, tomato purée/paste and maple syrup. It mixes with black beans for a great addition to dishes like bowls (page 86), tacos (page 104) and nachos (page 149).

avocado or olive oil, for frying
1 garlic clove, chopped
1 teaspoon smoked paprika
½ teaspoon ground cumin
1 x 400-g/14-oz. can black beans in their liquid
2 tablespoons tomato purée/paste
1 tablespoon pure maple syrup
60–120 ml/¼–½ cup water or vegetable stock/broth
salt, to taste

SERVES 4

Heat a thin layer of oil in a large pan with high sides over a medium-high heat. Add the garlic and spices and cook, stirring, for 1 minute.

Add the black beans with their liquid and stir to coat in the spices. Add the tomato purée/paste, maple syrup, season with salt and stir. Turn the heat to medium-low, cover and simmer for 10 minutes. Add some water or vegetable stock/broth if the mixture looks dry. Remove from heat and stand, covered, for 10 minutes before serving.

spicy tofu

This tofu is great to keep in the fridge to use in salads, grain bowls and stir-fries throughout the week. Sriracha is pretty spicy, but mellows when it's in the oven. If you prefer it milder, use half a tablespoon.

400-g/14-oz. block of extra firm tofu
3 tablespoons tamari
1 tablespoon sriracha
1 tablespoon sesame oil

baking tray, lined with baking parchment

SERVES 4-5

Remove the tofu from its packaging and drain. Wrap in paper towels and press with a weight, such as a heavy cookbook or baking tray, for 5–10 minutes to remove excess moisture. The dryer you get the tofu, the crispier it will become.

Preheat the oven to 200°C (400°F) Gas 6.

Meanwhile, put the tamari, sriracha and sesame oil in a medium-sized bowl. Mix together with a fork or whisk until well combined.

Cut the block of tofu into 2.5-cm/1-inch cubes and toss in the marinade. Let sit for about 15 minutes.

Scatter the tofu cubes onto the lined baking tray and bake in the preheated oven for 15 minutes. Flip the tofu cubes with a spatula and return to the oven for another 10–15 minutes until crisp and browned in places. Remove from the oven and leave to cool before serving.

SIMPLE DRESSINGS

herb dressing

This dressing is great if you have a bunch of leftover herbs you're looking to use up. It's totally adaptable to what you have and it gives a bright freshness to everything you eat it with.

If you want a creamier version of this, blend with 75 ml/⅓ cup soaked cashews or 2 tablespoons of Greek yogurt.

20 g/½ packed cup fresh parsley
20 g/½ packed cup fresh coriander/
   cilantro leaves and stems
10 basil leaves
1 garlic clove, peeled
1 tablespoon hemp seeds
1 tablespoon fresh lemon juice
60 ml/¼ cup olive oil

MAKES ABOUT 120 ML/½ CUP

Place all the ingredients along with 2 tablespoons of water in the bowl of a small food processor. Blend, scraping down the sides once or twice, for about 1–2 minutes, until smooth and very green.

honey mustard

Sweet, punchy and a little sharp. I love using
a combination of smooth and wholegrain
Dijon mustards to give this dressing a little
extra colour and texture.

4 tablespoons Dijon mustard (I used
    half smooth, half wholegrain)
2 tablespoons honey
2 tablespoons olive oil
1 teaspoon salt

sterilized jar with a lid (optional)

MAKES ABOUT 120 ML/^{1}/$_2$ CUP

Whisk all the ingredients together with
2 tablespoons of water in a small bowl, or place
all of the ingredients in the jar with a lid and
shake vigorously to combine. Add more water
to thin out, if desired.

basic vinaigrette

Simple, easy and necessary. I use this
one at least three times a week.

2 tablespoons vinegar (I like red wine or balsamic)
60 ml/¼ cup extra virgin olive oil
2 teaspoons Dijon mustard
¼ teaspoon salt
2–3 grinds of black pepper

sterilized jar with a lid (optional)

MAKES ABOUT 75 ML/^{1}/$_3$ CUP

Put everything together in the jar with a lid.
Add 1 tablespoon of water, pop the lid on, and
shake vigorously. Or, whisk everything together
in a small bowl. Add another tablespoon or so of
water until you reach the desired consistency.

NUTTY DRESSINGS

peanut dressing

Creamy with a little kick, this sauce is great for dipping vegetables and spring rolls in, or as the dressing for a noodle bowl.

2 tablespoons tamari
2 tablespoons natural (no sugar added) smooth peanut butter
1 tablespoon fresh lime juice
2.5-cm/1-inch piece of fresh ginger, grated or finely chopped
1 garlic clove, finely chopped
1 teaspoon chilli/chili paste

MAKES ABOUT 120 ML/¹/₂ CUP

In a small bowl, whisk together all the ingredients with 2 tablespoons of water or more as needed. Or, purée with a stick blender or in a small food processor until smooth.

tahini-lemon dressing

If you're new to tahini, give this classic dressing a try. It's great for when you're craving something creamy for salads, grain bowls and sandwiches.

50 g/¹/₄ cup tahini, mixed well
60 ml/¹/₄ cup warm water
juice of half a lemon, plus extra to taste
1 small garlic clove, finely chopped or grated
salt and freshly ground black pepper

sterilized jar with a lid (optional)

MAKES ABOUT 120 ML/¹/₂ CUP

Combine all the ingredients (including a pinch of salt and pepper) in the jar with a lid and shake vigorously. Or, whisk everything together in a small bowl. Taste for seasoning and add more salt and/or lemon juice if necessary.

tahini-ranch dressing

I used to love ranch dressing as a kid and wouldn't eat a salad that wasn't drowned in it. Today, I don't actually like the taste of most of the bottled varieties. This version has the requisite creaminess without the additives.

I use onion and garlic powder here, which aren't ingredients I use a lot in my cooking, but sometimes they're able to create that distinct flavour I'm looking for (see Everything Bagel Spice Mix page 41 and Buffalo-spiced Chickpeas page 93). The upside is, they're cheap and easy to find.

50 g/¼ cup tahini, mixed well
60 ml/¼ cup warm water
2 tablespoons finely chopped fresh chives
1 tablespoon finely chopped fresh parsley
1 teaspoon onion powder
1 teaspoon garlic powder
½ teaspoon dried dill
1 teaspoon maple syrup
freshly squeezed juice of half a lemon
½ teaspoon salt
few grinds of black pepper

MAKES ABOUT 175 ML/³/₄ CUP

In a small bowl, whisk together all the ingredients until well combined. Or, purée everything in a small food processor. Add a touch more water, if needed, to thin out to your desired consistency.

tahini-harissa dressing

Spicy, creamy and appropriate for dipping vegetables in, slathering on sandwiches or topping falafel with.

50 g/¼ cup tahini, mixed well
1 small garlic clove, peeled
1 teaspoon harissa paste
½ teaspoon salt
1 tablespoon fresh lemon juice

sterilized jar with a lid (optional)

MAKES ABOUT 120 ML/¹/₂ CUP

Blend everything together with 60 ml/¼ cup of water in a small food processor, or in the jar with a stick blender until smooth.

FLAVOUR-PACKED SAUCES

romesco sauce

I love this sauce for it's smoky richness and because it's made out of pantry staples.

60 g/½ cup cashews, soaked for at least an hour
200 g/1 cup roasted red peppers from a jar
1 garlic clove, peeled
2 tablespoons olive oil
1 tablespoon red wine vinegar
¼ teaspoon smoked Spanish paprika
¼ teaspoon cayenne pepper
½ teaspoon salt

MAKES ABOUT 295 ML/1¼ CUPS

Place all the ingredients in a small food processor and blend together until smooth. Taste for seasoning and add more salt as needed.

broccoli pesto

Make this pesto with that last crown of broccoli haunting your salad drawer.

1 small head of broccoli (including stems), chopped into small pieces
1 garlic clove, peeled
30 g/1 cup fresh basil, tightly packed
3–4 tablespoons olive oil
½ teaspoon nutritional yeast
¼ teaspoon salt, plus more to taste

MAKES ABOUT 350 ML/1½ CUPS

Cook the broccoli in a steamer basket or in a covered pan with a little boiling water for 3–5 minutes until tender. Drain and run under cold water. Combine the broccoli with the remaining ingredients in a small food processor and blend until smooth-ish. Adjust the seasoning to taste.

chermoula

With salty olives and the brightness of lemon zest and juice, this sauce gives a little lift to grains, roasted veg, fish or chicken.

120 ml/½ cup extra virgin olive oil
4 garlic cloves, roughly chopped
½ teaspoon ground coriander
½ teaspoon chilli flakes/hot red pepper flakes
¼ teaspoon ground cumin
¼ teaspoon paprika
15 g/½ cup fresh coriander/cilantro leaves and stems
15 g/⅓ cup fresh parsley leaves
½ teaspoon lemon zest
freshly squeezed juice of half a lemon
¼ teaspoon salt
35 g/⅓ cup whole pitted Kalamata olives, roughly chopped

MAKES ABOUT 235 ML/1 CUP

In a small saucepan, combine the oil and garlic over a medium-low heat. Cook for about 3–4 minutes until the garlic is sizzling, then let it sizzle for 1 minute.

Add the ground coriander, chilli flakes/hot red pepper flakes, cumin and paprika and stir. Turn off the heat and allow the mixture to cool in the pan.

Place the coriander/cilantro, parsley, lemon zest and juice, salt, olives and spiced garlic oil (along with the garlic) in a food processor (I use a mini one). Blend until everything is finely chopped and well combined.

Alternatively, finely chop all the ingredients and whisk together, adding the olive oil slowly.

CREAMY DIPS

basic avocado dip

This avocado dip is beyond simple to put together and adds a silky, vibrant green cloak to sautéed or roasted vegetables, grain bowls, and greens, and it makes a wonderful dip for quesadillas and sweet potato fries.

1 avocado, peeled and pitted
juice of half a lemon or lime
small handful of fresh coriander/
    cilantro leaves
sea salt, to taste

MAKES ABOUT 175-235 ML/³/₄-1 CUP

In a food processor or blender, place the avocado, lemon or lime juice, coriander/cilantro leaves and a good pinch of sea salt. Blend to a smooth purée.

Add water, a tablespoon at a time, and blend again until you reach the desired consistency – I like mine thick enough for a dip but thin enough to drizzle. Taste and add extra sea salt, if desired.

creamy chipotle dip

This sauce is becoming a fast favourite in our house. It's creamy, smoky and a little spicy. It's great on tacos and nachos (page 149).

75 g/⅓ cup tahini, mixed well
1 chipotle pepper in adobo sauce
    or ½ tablespoon chipotle paste
1 tablespoon adobo sauce from the pepper
    can (omit if using the paste)
1 tablespoon fresh lime juice
1 teaspoon maple syrup or honey
½ teaspoon salt
1 garlic clove, peeled

MAKES ABOUT 235 ML/1 CUP

Place all the ingredients in a food processor and blend together with 75 ml/⅓ cup of water until smooth. Add more water, if needed, to reach the desired consistency.

garlic yogurt dip

A more tasty alternative to sour cream.

215 g/1 cup Greek yogurt
1 garlic clove, chopped or finely grated
1 tablespoon olive oil, plus more to serve
¼ teaspoon salt
freshly ground black pepper, to taste

MAKES ABOUT 235 ML/1 CUP

In a small bowl, stir together the dip ingredients with a fork. Drizzle with additional olive oil and freshly ground black pepper, if desired.

CRUNCH & FLAVOUR TOPPINGS

caramelized onions

Caramelized onions make everything better, in my opinion. If I've made something that's turned out a little meh, the best way I can think to spruce it up is with a little helping of caramelized onions.

Best of all, caramelized onions are so simple to make with just a few very basic ingredients and some time.

I've provided an option for a spicy version, below, which takes caramelized onions to the next level – but feel free to stop with the first classic 5-ingredient version.

2 tablespoons olive oil
2 large red onions, thinly sliced
1 tablespoon balsamic vinegar
salt, to taste

SPICY OPTION
1 teaspoon chilli flakes/ hot red pepper flakes
1 teaspoon honey

SERVES 4-6

Heat the olive oil in your largest frying pan/skillet or Dutch oven over a medium heat. Add the sliced onions, season with salt and stir to combine.

Cook, stirring occasionally, for 15–20 minutes, reducing the heat to medium-low if the onions are browning quickly. If the mixture gets dry, add a splash of water to keep things from sticking.

Stir in the balsamic vinegar and cook for another 10–15 minutes, until the onions are softened, sweet and a little sticky. If you are going for the spicy option, stir in the chilli flakes/hot red pepper flakes and honey at the end of cooking.

walnut 'breadcrumbs'

This crunchy topping is reminiscent of Parmesan breadcrumbs. Use as a topping to add texture to pasta, salads, veggies, polenta or savoury oats.

2 tablespoons olive oil
1 garlic clove, finely chopped
½ teaspoon sea salt
140 g/1 cup walnut halves (or a combo of walnuts and cashews)
1 teaspoon nutritional yeast

baking tray, lined with baking parchment

SERVES 4-6

Preheat the oven to 180°C (350°F) Gas 4.

Combine all the ingredients in a small food processor. Pulse a few times to combine and roughly chop the nuts, until you have a coarse breadcrumb-like texture. (You can do this with a knife, too, it will just take a little longer.)

Spread the mixture out on the prepared baking tray. Bake in the preheated oven for 9–12 minutes until the walnuts are toasted and fragrant.

Allow to cool fully before using. Store in a sterilized jar in the fridge for up to 2 weeks.

dukkah

This spice and nut blend is a great way to add crunch and flavour to dishes. I love it combined with a few tablespoons of extra virgin olive oil as a dip for sourdough bread.

I use pistachios and almonds as my nut base, but you can use any combination of hazelnuts, macadamias, walnuts, and even throw in some pumpkin or sunflower seeds.

35 g/¼ cup pistachios, roughly chopped
35 g/¼ cup almonds, roughly chopped
1 tablespoon cumin seeds
1 tablespoon coriander seeds
1 tablespoon sesame seeds
1 teaspoon sea salt
1 teaspoon freshly ground black pepper
½ teaspoon chilli flakes/hot red pepper flakes

MAKES ABOUT 90 G/ ¾ CUP

Heat a large frying pan/skillet over a medium heat. Add the pistachios and almonds and dry toast them for about 5 minutes, tossing occasionally, until they're starting to turn golden and fragrant. Transfer to a plate.

In the same pan, toast the cumin seeds, coriander seeds and sesame seeds for about 2–4 minutes over a medium-low heat, until fragrant.

Combine the toasted nuts and seeds, salt, pepper and chilli flakes/hot red pepper flakes in the bowl of a small food processor and pulse carefully until just finely chopped – you don't want a fine powder, you're looking for pieces that lend a bit of crunch. Store in a sterilized glass jar in the fridge for up to a month.

savoury-sweet granola

I know granola on a green salad or as a savoury garnish sounds weird, but for me, it adds a good amount of crunch and flavour.

95 g/1 cup rolled oats
140 g/1 cup pumpkin seeds/pepitas
3 tablespoons flax seeds
1 tablespoon fresh thyme leaves
½ teaspoon salt
3 tablespoons olive oil
2 tablespoons honey

baking tray, lined with baking parchment

MAKES ABOUT 250 G/2 CUPS

Preheat the oven to 160°C (325°F) Gas 3.

Mix together the oats, pumpkin seeds/pepitas, flax seeds, thyme and salt in a medium bowl.

In another small bowl or pourable measuring cup, combine the olive oil and honey and stir together. Pour the olive oil mixture onto the oat mixture and stir until everything is well coated.

Spread the oats out on the prepared baking tray. Bake in the preheated oven for 35–40 minutes until golden. Rotate the tray halfway through the cooking time. Let the granola cool completely on the tray. Store in a sterilized glass jar in the fridge for up to a month.

coconut bacon bits

I'm not going to pretend that coconut is a doppleganger for bacon, but it does make a convincing plant-based stunt double. It hits the right crunchy, smoky and salty notes that can make a salad pop.

1 tablespoon olive oil
½ teaspoon maple syrup
¾ teaspoon smoked paprika
1 teaspoon salt
50 g/1 cup coconut flakes

baking tray, lined with baking parchment

MAKES ABOUT 50 G/1 CUP

Preheat the oven to 180°C (350°F) Gas 4.

In a medium bowl, whisk together the olive oil, maple syrup, smoked paprika and salt.

Add the coconut flakes to the bowl and stir to coat in the mixture.

Spread out on the prepared baking tray and bake in the preheated oven for 10 minutes. Allow to cool fully on the baking tray before serving. Store in a sterilized glass jar in the fridge for up to a month.

NUTRITION-PACKED ADD-ONS

garlic greens

If you have a big bunch of greens languishing in the fridge drawer, give them a clean and turn them into garlicky goodness. I like making a big batch to toss into grain bowls, soups and stews for a boost in leafy nutrients.

olive oil, for frying
3 garlic cloves, finely chopped
2 bunches of hearty greens like kale or Swiss chard, cleaned, stems removed*, and thinly sliced into ribbons
¼ teaspoon chilli flakes/hot red pepper flakes

SERVES 4

Heat a thin layer of olive oil in a large pan with high sides over a medium heat. Add the garlic and cook for 1 minute, stirring.

*If using Swiss chard, you can sauté the stems too. Finely chop the stems separately from the leaves. Add the stems to the hot pan first and cook for 2 minutes, stirring once or twice until softened. Add the leafy greens and cook for 2–3 minutes, stirring to distribute the heat, until wilted.

Remove from the heat and stir in the chilli flakes/hot red pepper flakes before serving.

pan-grilled broccoli

I like to slice broccoli almost like broccoli 'steaks' for this, cutting them lengthwise.

You want to partially caramelize the broccoli in the pan, so try not to toss or stir the pan in the first few minutes of cooking.

1–2 tablespoons olive oil
1 head of broccoli, with the tough bottom stem trimmed off and sliced into 1.5-cm/½-inch–2-cm/¾-inch thick pieces
2 garlic cloves, finely chopped or grated
salt, to taste

SERVES 4

Heat enough olive oil to cover the bottom of a large frying pan/skillet with a lid over a medium-high heat. Add the broccoli, distributing the pieces in an even layer. Season with salt.

Cover with a lid and cook for 4 minutes, without stirring, allowing the bottom to caramelize.

Add 120 ml/½ cup of water and the garlic and stir, flipping the broccoli slices as you do so. Cover again and cook for another 3 minutes until tender and caramelized on both sides.

5-seed slaw

This colourful slaw gets extra crunch and flavour from the addition of toasted seeds. You can make this the day before you intend to serve and store it in the fridge.

1 tablespoon sesame seeds
1 tablespoon pumpkin seeds/pepitas
1 tablespoon sunflower seeds
1 teaspoon cumin seeds
1 tablespoon poppy seeds
1 teaspoon Dijon mustard
juice of ½ lemon
2 tablespoons olive oil
¼ head of red cabbage, finely sliced using a mandoline or knife
60 g/1 cup kale, stems removed and shredded
1 large carrot, grated or peeled with a julienne peeler
small handful of fresh coriander/cilantro or parsley leaves, roughly chopped
salt, to taste

SERVES 4

Heat a medium frying pan/skillet over a medium heat. Add the sesame seeds, pumpkin seeds/pepitas, sunflower seeds, cumin seeds and poppy seeds. Dry toast for about 5–6 minutes, until fragrant and the sesame seeds are beginning to brown. Transfer the seeds to a plate and allow time to cool fully.

In a large bowl, combine the Dijon mustard, lemon juice and olive oil. Season with salt to taste and whisk quickly with a fork.

In the same bowl, add the cabbage, kale, carrot and fresh herbs and toss to evenly coat everything in the dressing. Add the toasted cooled seeds and toss again.

BREAKFASTS

Mornings are brighter, livelier and more fun with a good breakfast. These are some of my favourite dishes to get me moving or encourage me to linger over another cup of coffee (depending on the day).

green smoothie bowl
with peanut butter & banana

I know smoothies aren't the first thing that come to mind when you think of a comforting meal, but hear me out on this one.

I never used to crave smoothies for breakfast – I preferred crunch, texture and, you know, chewing. Slurping something quickly through a straw isn't a meal to me.

Smoothie bowls, on the other hand, are entirely different in my mind. The change of vessel allows your smoothie to be enjoyed sitting at the table, spoon in hand, with copious amounts of toppings for added bite and flavour.

For smoothie bowls, I look for a thicker texture, so blending can take a little longer than normal, but it's worth the wait.

This one is refreshing yet rich, peanut buttery and creamy in a way that makes me crave it nearly every hot summer morning.

120 ml/½ cup almond milk
220 g/1½ cups frozen spinach (or 2 big handfuls of the fresh stuff)
1 frozen banana, broken into pieces
75 g/½ cup frozen mango chunks
1–2 tablespoons smooth peanut butter

OPTIONAL ADD-INS
1 teaspoon coconut oil
1 tablespoon flax seeds
1 tablespoon chia seeds

OPTIONAL TOPPINGS
granola
cacao nibs
coconut flakes
extra peanut butter
fresh fruit

SERVES 1

Pour the almond milk into the base of a blender. Add the spinach, banana and mango and start to blend at high speed. As the mixture is blending, pause once or twice to scrape down the sides with a rubber spatula to make sure that everything is well incorporated.

When the mixture is smooth, stop the blender, then add the peanut butter and any optional add-ins.

Blend again until everything is smooth and thick. Pour the smoothie into a bowl to serve and finish with your chosen toppings.

chickpea socca pancakes
with mushrooms & thyme

Socca are crispy-edged Mediterranean pancakes made with chickpea (gram) flour. They are perfect for topping with savoury or sweet ingredients.

Slightly thicker than crepes, socca have a nutty-sweet flavour and a high protein content which makes them more of a wholesome, filling meal. They can be eaten for a fancy-ish breakfast or a laid-back dinner with a big green salad on the side.

In this recipe, I pair the socca with earthy mushrooms, but you can play around with whatever fillings you'd like. I also like these with roasted tomatoes and a fried egg, or coconut yogurt and sliced fruit. My sweet socca pancakes (page 169) can be eaten for breakfast or dessert.

125 g/1 cup chickpea (gram) flour
½ teaspoon salt
olive oil or grass-fed butter, for frying

FOR THE MUSHROOMS
1 tablespoon olive oil or grass-fed butter
5 sprigs of fresh thyme, leaves removed from the stems
225 g/8 oz. cremini mushrooms, sliced
1 garlic clove, finely minced or grated
salt and freshly ground black pepper, to taste

OPTIONAL TOPPINGS
grated Parmesan or Gruyère
a fried egg

SERVES 2

Put the chickpea (gram) flour, salt and 295 ml/1¼ cups water into a large bowl and mix together with a whisk or a fork until well combined into a smooth batter. Leave to stand at room temperature for at least 10 minutes.

Meanwhile, heat a thin layer of oil or butter in a large frying pan/skillet over a high heat. Add the thyme leaves and mushrooms and cook, stirring occasionally, for 2–3 minutes until the mushrooms soften and are slightly golden. Reduce the heat to medium, then add the garlic and cook for 1 minute more. Season to taste with salt and pepper. Keep the mushrooms warm in a low oven or in a covered dish while you cook the pancakes.

Heat the olive oil or butter in another small frying pan/skillet over a medium heat. Add approximately 60–75 ml/¼ – scant ⅓ cup of the socca batter to the warm pan. Swirl it around so that it covers the base of the pan. Fry for about 2–3 minutes, until the batter begins to form bubbles. Flip the pancake with a spatula and cook for another 1–2 minutes on the other side.

Repeat with the remaining batter. This should make you about 4 small socca pancakes in total. Serve with the mushrooms and any additional toppings you like.

chai & turmeric porridge

I'm always trying to sneak turmeric into as many dishes as I can. This root has some serious nutritional cred, with a slew of studies backing its anti-inflammatory properties. And with its vibrant yellow-gold hue, I can't help but be drawn to it. Using it alongside chai spices in my morning oats is an easy way to fit it into my day.

This porridge is made with a combination of rolled oats and buckwheat groats. It should be noted that buckwheat isn't a wheat or grain at all, it's a naturally gluten-free seed that's high in magnesium, iron and vitamin B6.

If you can't find buckwheat, you can use all regular rolled oats instead. This porridge is also naturally sweetened with bananas for a spiced banana bread vibe, but if you're not feeling that, you can use an apple grated on a box grater. Add along with any juices to the porridge at the same time that you would add the banana.

45 g/½ cup rolled oats
80 g/½ cup buckwheat groats (untoasted)
½ teaspoon ground cinnamon
½ teaspoon ground turmeric
½ teaspoon ground ginger
¼ teaspoon ground cardamom
¼ teaspoon ground nutmeg
⅛ teaspoon ground cloves
salt, to taste
475 ml/2 cups boiling water
235 ml/1 cup almond or coconut milk, plus extra to serve if needed
½ teaspoon vanilla extract
1 banana, sliced

TO SERVE
toasted flaked/slivered almonds
chopped figs, berries or extra banana

SERVES 2

Combine the oats and buckwheat in a medium saucepan with a lid. Add all the spices, season with salt to taste and stir until everything is well mixed together.

Pour in the boiling water, almond or coconut milk and vanilla, then bring to the boil.

Reduce to a simmer and cook with the lid on for about 10 minutes, stirring occasionally until the oats are soft and most of the liquid has been absorbed.*

Stir in the banana slices and cook for an additional 10 minutes, until they're softened and smell sweet. Serve with additional almond milk and a topping of toasted flaked/slivered almonds and fresh fruit.

*Alternatively, to save time in the morning you can prepare the oats the night before: simmer for 5 minutes, then remove from the heat and cover with a lid. Let the oats soak overnight at room temperature or in the fridge. In the morning, add a sliced banana to the oats. Bring back up to a bubble, adding a little more water or almond milk to loosen. Once heated through and creamy and the bananas are fragrant, you're ready to go.

coconut bircher muesli
with berry compote

I love making this breakfast in the spring and summer, when hot porridge or oatmeal doesn't feel quite right. Bircher muesli is a combination of oats, fruit and liquid that's been soaked overnight until the oats are softened and more easily digestible. It's pretty much the same thing as 'overnight oats', but with grated apple for sweetness, tartness and texture.

Be sure to include the juices from the grated apple in your oat mixture, for extra flavour.

When you're ready for breakfast, all that's left to do is add your chosen yogurt and fruit topping.

The addition of the stewed berry compote makes this an extra special breakfast. It's easy to make from frozen berries any time of year for added antioxidant-rich goodness.

95 g/1 cup rolled oats
235 ml/1 cup coconut or
   almond milk
1 medium sweet apple
   (such as Honeycrisp or
   Pink Lady), grated
1 tablespoon flax seeds
1 teaspoon maple syrup
¼ teaspoon ground
   cinnamon
pinch of salt
1 teaspoon lemon juice

FOR THE BERRY COMPOTE
300 g/1½ cups mixed fresh
   or frozen berries (I love
   a mixture of raspberries,
   blueberries and/or
   blackberries)
1 teaspoon maple syrup
pinch of ground cinnamon

1 teaspoon chia seeds
   (optional, although you
   will have to extend the
   cooking time by a little
   if you leave them out)

OPTIONAL TOPPINGS
toasted nuts and seeds
toasted coconut flakes
hemp seeds
almond butter
yogurt

*2 medium-sized sterilized
jars with lids*

SERVES 2

In a medium bowl, mix the muesli ingredients together until well combined. Portion between the two jars, cover with the lids and refrigerate overnight. (This gives the oats plenty of time to soften and soak up the flavours).

Make the berry compote straight after preparing the oats. Combine the mixed berries, maple syrup and cinnamon with 120 ml/½ cup water in a small saucepan. Bring to a boil over a medium heat, then stir in the chia seeds (if using). Reduce to a simmer and cook for about 7–8 minutes, until the liquid has reduced and the mixture is taking on a jammy consistency. If you are not using chia seeds, the mixture will need cooking for about 10–13 minutes. Allow to cool, then place in the fridge overnight with the oats.

Serve the bircher muesli layered with or topped with the berry compote and any additional desired toppings.

SWEET TOASTS

I love the creativity that comes from combining a few things on a piece of bread. The following are intended more as suggestions than recipes, I hope they inspire you to find new favourite combinations.

peanut butter & berry

Like PB&J – but way better.

2 slices of bread
2 tablespoons peanut
    butter
50–60 g/⅓–½ cup
    fresh berries

or thawed frozen
    berries
honey, to serve
hemp seeds, to serve

SERVES 1

Toast the bread to your desired toastiness. Slather on peanut butter. Top with berries, a drizzle of honey and a sprinkle of hemp seeds.

banana & seed

Natural sweetness with a side of crunch.

2 slices of bread
2 tablespoons almond
    butter
1 banana, sliced into
    rounds

½ teaspoon hemp
    seeds
½ teaspoon chia seeds
1 teaspoon pumpkin
    seeds/pepitas

SERVES 1

Toast the bread to your desired toastiness. Spread with a generous amount of almond butter. Top with banana slices and sprinkle on the seeds.

hazelnut choc spread

This recipe makes more chocolate spread than needed for 1 serving, but it keeps well in the fridge for 2 weeks. It will save time if you can get the hazelnuts without skins on.

130 g/1 cup hazelnuts
2 tablespoons melted
    coconut oil
2 tablespoons maple
    syrup or honey
2 tablespoons cocoa
    powder
1 teaspoon vanilla
    extract

pinch of sea salt
2 slices of bread
sliced strawberries,
    to serve
toasted hazelnuts,
    roughly chopped,
    to serve (optional)

SERVES 1

Preheat the oven to 180°C (350°F) Gas 4.

Spread the hazelnuts out on a dry baking tray. Pop in the preheated oven for 5 minutes, shake the tray and return to the oven for another 5 minutes until lightly toasted. If the skins are on the hazelnuts, cover the baking tray with a kitchen towel and allow to cool for about 5–10 minutes.

Remove the skins by rolling your hands over the towel covering the nuts. You're trying to jostle them enough so the skins begin to fall away. Getting about three quarters off is a win here, some are very stubborn. Transfer to a food processor or high speed blender and process for about 5–8 minutes. Push beyond the fine powder until you get a denser, softened nut butter.

Add the melted coconut oil, syrup or honey, cocoa powder, vanilla and sea salt and blend for 1–2 minutes until fairly smooth.

Toast the bread, then spread with the chocolate spread and top with sliced strawberries and chopped toasted hazelnuts, if desired.

fig & tahini toast

This toast is on repeat in my kitchen come September (and even late August) when figs start arriving at my local market.

Nutty, sweet and just the tiniest bit salty, this is one of the most glorious ways to enjoy figs. I like to sprinkle a few chopped pistachios on here if I have them to hand.

2 slices of bread
2–3 tablespoons tahini
3–4 fresh figs, sliced

TO SERVE
honey
pinch of flaky sea salt,
  such as Maldon
chopped pistachios

SERVES 1

Toast the bread to your liking. Smear with tahini and top with sliced figs. Drizzle with honey and sprinkle with sea salt and chopped pistachios to serve.

SAVOURY TOASTS

These toasts make properly satisfying, substantial breakfasts, but also work as great easy dinners, too. I love to use a campagne loaf from Bien Cuit or sourdough miche from Runner & Stone (both of which are my local Brooklyn gems), and sprouted multigrain from Ezekiel, but really any fresh sturdy bread with a good crust will do.

roasted carrot & hummus

The new avocado toast? My vote is for hummus and roasted veggies.

2 slices of bread
1 garlic clove, cut in half
60 g/¼ cup Hummus (page 144)
2–4 teaspoons Dukkah (page 20)
2 teaspoons freshly chopped parsley
olive oil, for drizzling
salt and freshly ground black pepper, to taste

FOR THE ROASTED CARROTS
4 carrots
splash of olive oil
sea salt, to taste

SERVES 2

Preheat the oven to 220°C (425°F) Gas 7.

Peel and roughly chop the carrots and toss with the oil and a big pinch of salt. Place on a baking sheet and roast in the preheated oven for 25–30 minutes until golden and brown at the edges.

Toast the bread to your liking. Rub the warm bread with the half garlic clove.

Spread the bread with hummus and top with roasted carrots, dukkah and parsley. Drizzle with olive oil and season with salt and pepper.

peas & spinach

Bright green peas on toast somehow seem to set any morning on the right track.

I love adding a little salty garnish like capers, goat's cheese or feta to offset the natural sweetness of the peas, but just a small sprinkle of sea salt can help you with that, too.

olive oil for frying, plus extra for serving
1 garlic clove, finely chopped
125 g/1 cup frozen peas, thawed
large handful of baby spinach
1 teaspoon lemon juice, plus extra to taste
2 large slices (or 4 small) of sourdough
1 garlic clove, cut in half
salt and freshly ground black pepper, to taste
goat's cheese or capers (optional), to serve

SERVES 2

In a medium frying pan/skillet, heat a thin layer of oil over a medium heat. Add the garlic and stir-fry for 20–30 seconds before adding the peas and spinach. Cook, stirring regularly, until everything is warmed through and the spinach has wilted, about 3 minutes. Season with salt and lemon juice and remove from the heat.

Mash the pan contents lightly with a fork or potato masher, or pulse everything in a food processor or blender. You're looking for a texture that is somewhere between a smooth purée and completely whole, so that the peas can stay atop the toast without rolling off.

Meanwhile, toast the bread to your desired shade of toastiness. Rub the warm bread with the cut sides of the garlic clove.

Spread the pea mixture on the toast. Top with goat's cheese and/or capers and black pepper.

tomato & white beans

This dish is all about creating something warming and satisfying from very little – whatever you have in your pantry will work. I've made it using diced fresh tomatoes, jarred tomato pasta sauce and whole canned tomatoes (which I roughly broke up with a flat-ended wooden spoon), all with good results.

2 tablespoons olive oil
3 large garlic cloves (or 5 small), finely chopped
1 tablespoon finely chopped fresh sage
1 x 400-g/14-oz. can chopped tomatoes
1 x 400-g/14-oz. can white beans, drained and rinsed
chilli flakes/hot red pepper flakes (optional)
salt, to taste
2–3 slices of toasted bread, flatbread or pita, to serve

SERVES 2-3

Heat the olive oil in a medium frying pan/skillet over a medium heat. Add the garlic and sage and sauté for 30 seconds until fragrant.

Stir in the tomatoes and white beans, then season with salt. Reduce the heat to low and cook, covered, for 10–15 minutes, stirring once or twice. Add a small splash of water if the pan dries out at any point.

Stir in chilli flakes/hot red pepper flakes (if using) and remove from the heat. Serve warm with toasted bread of your choice.

everything avocado toast

One of my first jobs was working as a counter server at a Long Island bagel store. Here I worked the griddle, perfected my sunny-side-up egg technique, learned the art of making iced coffee and had unlimited access to everything bagels.

Everything bagels are famous in New York – they're covered in a flavourful combination of seeds and alliums and in my opinion, they're the best type of bagel.

Even though at the end of the shift my hair smelled like bacon and my shoes were filled with poppy seeds and garlic granules, I never got sick of those everything bagels.

When I lived in Sydney, it was pretty much impossible to find a bagel comparable to a New York bagel, so my Everything Bagel Spice Mix became an easy way to get a little taste of home.

Combined with avocado and spring onions/scallions, it's pretty much all of my favourite breakfasts rolled into one.

2 large (or 4 small) slices of sourdough, whole grain or sprouted grain bread
1 avocado, peeled, pitted and roughly chopped
1 spring onion/scallion, finely sliced
Everything Bagel Spice Mix (recipe below)

SERVES 2

Toast the bread to your liking, then top with the avocado, dividing it evenly between each slice. Use a fork to mash the avocado, pressing it into the toast. Sprinkle with the sliced spring onion/scallion and finally with some of the Everything Bagel Spice Mix.

everything bagel spice mix

1 tablespoon sesame seeds
1 tablespoon poppy seeds
1 tablespoon dried garlic granules
1 tablespoon onion powder or dried onion
2 teaspoons sea salt

MAKES ABOUT 4 TABLESPOONS

Toast the sesame seeds in a dry frying pan/skillet over a medium-low heat for about 5 minutes until turning golden. Watch them carefully, as they can burn easily. Remove from heat and allow to cool for about 5 minutes.

Put all the seeds and flavourings together in a small jar and shake to combine. The spice mix will keep for up to 6 months in the jar with a lid. It's also a great flavour and texture boost on salads, quinoa/grains, hummus, eggs and baked into savoury breads or muffins.

vegan breakfast sandwich

I have a deep love for New York delis and the egg breakfast sandwiches that are served in them. It's something that can't quite be replicated out of the Long Island/NYC/New Jersey area – like bagels and pizza by the slice.

When I began thinking of a totally plant-based version of a breakfast sandwich, I couldn't really wrap my head around it when I took away the egg and the cheese. But then I thought about the essence of a good breakfast sandwich, which is warming, rich and filling.

This breakfast sandwich is that. It's got creamy elements, as well as substantial carb-y ones, and has enough tang from harissa and barbecue sauce to keep it interesting.

It's also lovely topped with a fried egg, if that's your vibe.

1 butternut squash, peeled
1 avocado, peeled and pitted
1 tablespoon freshly chopped coriander/cilantro (optional)
4 English muffins (I love the Ezekiel sprouted ones)
salt, to taste

TO SERVE
Tahini-harissa Dressing (page 13)
barbecue sauce

a baking sheet, oiled

SERVES 4

Preheat the oven to 200°C (400°F) Gas 6.

Slice the neck or handle part of the butternut squash into 1.5-cm/½-inch thick rounds (save the hollowed-out base of the squash for another recipe). Spread the rounds out on the prepared baking sheet and season with salt to taste. Roast in the preheated oven for 30 minutes, flipping about halfway through, until golden and tender.

In a medium bowl, lightly mash the avocado with a pinch of salt and the chopped coriander/cilantro (if using).

When you're ready to serve, split and toast the English muffins. Spread the Tahini-Harissa Dressing on one half of each, top that with a butternut round or two and drizzle with barbecue sauce.

Spread the mashed avocado on the other half of each English muffin and sandwich everything together.

sweet brekkie
sweet potato

Here are two recipes to help you break out of a breakfast rut. I tend to go through phases where I eat the same thing for breakfast for a month straight and am suddenly very ready to mix it up. A baked sweet potato is the perfect remedy.

These recipes are for one serving and one sweet potato, but I'd suggest baking a few sweet potatoes at the same time so you have them ready to go for the week. Mix it up with sweet and savoury fillings.

1 small sweet potato, scrubbed clean and poked with a fork a couple of times
1–2 teaspoons maple syrup
1 tablespoon almond butter
pinch of ground cinnamon
2 big spoonfuls of coconut yogurt or yogurt of your choice
handful of fresh berries
handful of granola

SERVES 1

Preheat the oven to 200°C (400°F) Gas 6.

Put the sweet potato on the oven rack and bake in the preheated oven for about 45–60 minutes, until soft to the touch. Allow to cool a little.
Note: You can do this step ahead of time and make a whole batch for the week, then reheat them in the microwave or oven right before serving.

Slice the warm potato open lengthwise and lightly mash the flesh with a fork.

Drizzle with maple syrup and almond butter, then sprinkle with cinnamon. Top with coconut yogurt, berries and granola to finish.

savoury brekkie
sweet potato

1 small sweet potato, scrubbed clean and poked with a fork a couple of times
½ avocado, peeled and pitted
1 tablespoon freshly chopped coriander/cilantro
salt, to taste
pinch of chilli flakes/
hot red pepper flakes or dash of hot sauce, plus extra to serve
olive oil
40 g/¼ cup canned black beans, drained and rinsed
fried or poached egg, to serve (optional)

SERVES 1

Preheat the oven to 200°C (400°F) Gas 6.

Put the sweet potato on the oven rack and bake in the preheated oven for about 45–60 minutes, until soft to the touch. Allow to cool a little.
Note: You can do this step ahead of time and make a whole batch for the week, then reheat them in the microwave or oven right before serving.

In a bowl, roughly mash the avocado flesh with the coriander/cilantro, a little salt and chilli flakes/hot red pepper flakes or hot sauce.

Slice the warm potato open lengthwise and lightly mash the flesh with a fork.

Top with a drizzle of olive oil, the mashed avocado and black beans. Serve with extra hot sauce and/or a fried or poached egg, if desired.

SOUPS & STEWS

As far as cosy staples go, a hearty soup or stew is the most essential. They score extra points because most get better the longer they sit, so they're perfect for making ahead. What is more comforting than a meal that's already made?

spring vegetable soup

While this soup works on its own, I highly recommend serving it with
a scoop of freshly made or store-bought pesto on top. It adds a herbaceous
boost that matches up perfectly with thawing temperatures.

olive oil, for frying
1 onion, finely diced
2 leeks, white and light
    green parts only,
    thinly sliced into
    half-moons
3 garlic cloves, finely
    chopped
10 sprigs of fresh
    thyme, leaves
    removed from stems
1 tablespoon finely
    chopped fresh
    parsley leaves
    and stems
950 ml/4 cups
    vegetable stock/
    broth
1 x 400-g/14-oz. can
    white beans, drained
    and rinsed

1 courgette/zucchini,
    cut into small,
    bite-sized pieces
125 g/1 cup frozen peas,
    thawed
1 carrot, peeled and
    shaved into ribbons
130 g/2 cups kale,
    stems removed and
    shredded
salt, to taste
Broccoli Pesto (page 14)
    or store-bought
    pesto, to serve

SERVES 4-6

Heat a thin layer of olive oil in a large saucepan
or Dutch oven over a medium heat. Add the onion
and leeks, season with salt and cook, stirring
occasionally, for 7–8 minutes until softened.

Stir in the garlic, thyme leaves and parsley and
cook for 1 minute.

Pour in the vegetable stock/broth, then turn up
the heat and bring everything to a boil. Add the
beans, then turn down the heat and simmer
uncovered for 15 minutes, stirring a few times.

Add the courgette/zucchini and cook for another
3 minutes until the courgette/zucchini is tender
but not mushy.

Stir in the peas, carrot ribbons and shredded kale
and remove from the heat. Let the soup stand for
about 5 minutes to let the flavours mingle.

Pour into bowls and serve with a big scoop of
pesto stirred into each.

creamy roasted tomato soup

A rich and creamy tomato soup that will perk up any rainy day.

Canned tomatoes actually work best for this recipe and roasting them builds that appealing sweet and savoury combination of flavours.

Don't be intimidated by the cashew cream, it's really simple if you have a stick blender or food processor and adds protein and a little something special to your bowl.

60 g/½ cup cashew nuts
2 x 400-g/14-oz. cans whole tomatoes
6–8 garlic cloves (depending on size), peeled and crushed with the side of a wide knife
olive oil, for frying
1 onion, finely diced
1 tablespoon tomato purée/paste
475 ml/2 cups vegetable stock/broth
salt and freshly ground black pepper, to taste
good-quality bread, for dipping

a medium roasting pan, generously drizzled with olive oil

SERVES 4

Place the cashews in a container and pour over enough cold water to completely submerge. Let soak for at least 1 hour at room temperature.

Preheat the oven to 200°C (400°F) Gas 6.

Pour the canned tomatoes out onto the prepared roasting pan (with all the juices) and break apart with your hands. Note: be careful as they will splash your clothes – I recommend an apron or an old t-shirt for this job.

Scatter the tomatoes with the garlic and season with salt. Bake in the preheated oven for 40 minutes until bubbling and the juices have slightly reduced but are still plentiful.

Meanwhile, in a large saucepan over a medium heat, warm enough olive oil to cover the base. Add the onion and cook, stirring occasionally, for about 10 minutes until softened.

Add the tomato purée/paste and cook for 2 more minutes. Pour in the vegetable stock/broth and roasted tomatoes (along with the garlic) and simmer for about 10–15 minutes. Remove from the heat.

Blend the soup with a stick blender or in batches in a food processor until smooth.

Drain the soaked cashews and blend together with a fresh 120 ml/½ cup of water with a stick blender or in a food processor until creamy.

Portion the soup into bowls and swirl in a little cashew cream to each. Serve with plenty of freshly ground black pepper and nice bread on the side for dipping.

leek, cauliflower & fennel soup

Creamy, flavourful and a little on the beige side, this soup is a cosy winter favourite of mine. Roasted fennel is a very special ingredient in itself (tasting totally different from raw), it infuses this soup with mild, sweet notes. The colour of the soup can feel a little drab, so I toss in a couple of handfuls of bright green baby spinach at the very end of cooking (before blending) almost purely for cosmetic reasons.

1 head of cauliflower, cut into small florets
1 large bulb of fennel, sliced into 1.5-cm/ ½-inch thick pieces, long green stems and fronds cut off and set aside for garnishing
olive or avocado oil, for frying
1 leek, white and light green parts only, thinly sliced into half-moons
3 garlic cloves, finely chopped
1½ teaspoons fresh thyme leaves
950 ml/4 cups vegetable stock/ broth
2 handfuls of baby spinach (optional)
salt and freshly ground black pepper, to taste
lemon wedges, to serve
good-quality bread, to serve

2 baking trays, both greased with a thin layer of olive or avocado oil

SERVES 4

Preheat the oven to 200°C (400°F) Gas 6.

Scatter the cauliflower florets onto one of the prepared baking trays and the sliced fennel onto the other. Season to taste with salt and roast in the preheated oven for about 20–25 minutes, until both vegetables are golden and tender.

Meanwhile, in a large saucepan, heat enough oil to cover the base over a medium heat. Add the sliced leek and a pinch of salt and cook for about 10 minutes, stirring occasionally, until softened and starting to turn golden. Stir in the garlic and cook for another minute. Add the thyme leaves and let it sizzle for 30 seconds.

Stir in the roasted cauliflower and fennel followed by the vegetable stock/broth. Turn up the heat to bring to a boil, then reduce the heat and simmer for about 5 minutes. If you're adding spinach, stir it in now and allow to wilt. Remove from the heat and allow to cool for 5 minutes.

Blend the soup with a stick blender or in batches in a food processor until smooth. Pour into bowls and serve with lemon wedges for squeezing over, ground black pepper and good bread. Garnish with the reserved fennel fronds, if you like.

green Thai soup

Most weeks, I automatically buy broccoli because it's affordable and so very good for you. Unfortunately, I find myself in broccoli ruts quite often – tiring of roasting, steaming and sautéing it.

This soup is perfect for all green vegetable ruts. It has Thai spices from my secret flavour weapon, green curry paste, creaminess from coconut milk, and it's packed to the brim with green vegetables. You can use spinach (fresh or frozen) or Swiss chard in place of kale, or throw in that random kohlrabi that you don't know what to do with – it's all good in this soup.

I prefer to serve this mostly puréed, with a helping of brown rice for texture and bulk, but you can skip the blender and keep it chunky or serve it with cubes of roasted sweet potato instead of rice.

olive or avocado oil,
   for frying
1 leek, white and light
   green parts only, thinly
   sliced
salt, to taste
2 garlic cloves, finely
   chopped
2 tablespoons Thai green
   curry paste
1 broccoli crown with
   stems, chopped into
   small pieces
475 ml/2 cups boiling water
1 courgette/zucchini,
   roughly chopped
125 g/1 cup frozen peas
2 large handfuls of kale,
   stems removed and
   roughly chopped
1 x 400-g/14-oz. can coconut
   milk (I use full fat)
5 sprigs of fresh coriander/
   cilantro with stems
   (plus more for serving),
   roughly chopped
cooked brown rice, to serve
   (optional)

SERVES 3-4

In a large saucepan with a lid, heat a good glug of oil over a medium-high heat. Add the leek, season to taste with salt and cook, stirring occasionally, for about 5–7 minutes, until the leek has softened.

Add the garlic and fry for another minute. Stir in the curry paste and cook for another minute. Add the broccoli and boiling water to the pan and stir.

Bring to a simmer and add the courgette/zucchini. Cover the pan and simmer for about 5 minutes until the vegetables are tender.

Stir in the peas and kale, cover, and cook for another 1–2 minutes until the kale has wilted. Turn off the heat and stir in coconut milk (reserving a little to garnish) and coriander/cilantro.

If blending, use a stick blender or purée in batches in a food processor until mostly smooth.

Served the soup in bowls with extra coriander/cilantro, a drizzle of the reserved coconut milk and a portion of cooked brown rice, if desired.

ginger coconut broth
veggies & noodles

This falls somewhere between a soup, a curry and a brothy ramen bowl. With ginger, chilli and garlic flavours it often hits the spot when I'm looking for something that I can slurp a big bowl of without it weighing me down.

FOR THE BROTH

2 teaspoons avocado oil

4 garlic cloves, finely chopped or grated

2 tablespoons grated fresh ginger

1 x 400-g/14-oz. can coconut milk (I use full fat)

2 tablespoons tamari

120 ml/½ cup water or vegetable stock/broth

¼ teaspoon chilli flakes/ hot red pepper flakes (optional)

ADD-INS

120–170 g/4–6 oz. soba noodles

1 courgette/zucchini, peeled or spiralized into noodles or cut into julienne

1 carrot, spiralized into noodles or cut into julienne

130 g/1 cup shelled frozen edamame beans, thawed

SERVES 2–3

Cook the soba noodles in boiling water according to the package instructions. (The 100% buckwheat soba noodles I use usually take about 8 minutes.)

While the soba noodles are cooking, heat the avocado oil in a large saucepan or high-sided frying pan/skillet over a medium-high heat. Add the garlic and ginger and let them sizzle for about 30–60 seconds until fragrant, but not browning.

Add the coconut milk and tamari and stir. Add the water or vegetable stock/broth and chilli flakes/hot red pepper flakes (if using).

Bring to a simmer, then stir in the courgette/zucchini, carrot and edamame beans and let everything warm through for about 2 minutes. Remove from heat.

Divide the cooked soba noodles between bowls and pour the hot broth and veggies over to serve.

pumpkin coconut soup
with warming spices

This spiced soup is a great warmer for the first chilly weeks of fall/autumn. With its slight sweetness, bold spice combination and nutty grains to serve, it feels grounding and cosy while setting itself apart from other plain pumpkin soups.

I've even eaten it for breakfast because it can kind of feel like an exotic porridge.

It's really nice served with some fresh coriander/cilantro leaves and a squeeze of fresh lime juice, if you've got it.

1 tablespoon avocado or coconut oil
1 onion, diced
3 garlic cloves, finely chopped
2 tablespoons grated fresh ginger
1 teaspoon ground cumin
½ teaspoon ground cinnamon
½ teaspoon cayenne pepper
¼ teaspoon ground nutmeg
pinch of ground allspice
2 carrots, roughly chopped
450 g/3½ cups diced pumpkin or 2 x 400-g/14-oz. cans pumpkin or butternut squash purée
475 ml/2 cups boiling water
1 x 400-g/14-oz. can coconut milk (I use full fat)
salt, to taste
135 g/1 cup cooked brown rice, barley or farro, to serve

SERVES 4-6

In a large saucepan with a lid, heat the oil over a medium heat. Add the onion, season with salt and cook, stirring occasionally, for about 6–8 minutes, until the onion is turning golden.

Add the garlic, ginger, cumin, cinnamon, cayenne pepper, nutmeg and allspice and cook for 1 minute, stirring everything frequently.

Add the carrots and pumpkin and season with salt. Pour in the boiling water and stir. Cover and cook for about 10 minutes. Remove the lid and simmer for another 10 minutes, until the vegetables are tender.

Turn off the heat and stir in the coconut milk. Blend with a stick blender or in batches in a food processor until smooth. Divide the soup into bowls and serve with a scoop of cooked brown rice, barley or farro in each.

carrot soup *with crispy miso lentils*

The star of this dish is the miso lentils. They're crunchy and umami and everything I want in a soup garnish.

The key is to make sure your lentils are cooked 'al dente' and are well drained and fairly dry before going into a hot pan. I find that leaving them to drain in a colander for 10-15 minutes, giving the colander a shake or two and lightly blotting with a clean kitchen cloth works well.

450 g/1 lb. carrots, roughly chopped in half and again lengthwise, into thumb-sized pieces
1 tablespoon avocado or olive oil
1 teaspoon ground cumin
3 garlic cloves, skins on and crushed with the side of a wide knife
950 ml/4 cups low-sodium vegetable stock/broth
1 tablespoon fresh lemon juice
salt and freshly ground black pepper

FOR THE MISO LENTILS
95 g/½ cup dried black or French/du Puy lentils, soaked for an hour or overnight and drained
1 tablespoon white miso paste
2 tablespoons avocado oil
extra virgin olive oil, to serve
Dukkah (page 20), to serve

SERVES 4

Preheat the oven to 200°C (400°F) Gas 6.

In a large bowl, mix together the carrots, oil and cumin and season with salt. Toss until everything is coated. Arrange on a large baking tray (or divide between two trays, so as not to crowd the carrots) with the garlic cloves. Roast in the preheated oven for about 25–30 minutes until softened and golden.

Meanwhile, put the lentils in a medium saucepan with 475 ml/2 cups of water and a pinch of salt. Bring to a boil, then reduce the heat to medium–low, cover with a lid and cook for about 18–20 minutes. You want them al dente with a little bit of bite. Drain the lentils well, keeping them in the colander for at least 10 minutes.

Once the carrots are cooked, place in a blender or food processor. Remove the roasted garlic cloves from their skins and add those to the blender. Pour in the vegetable stock/broth and blend until smooth (you may need to do this in batches).

Pour the soup into a clean saucepan and stir in the lemon juice. Bring everything to a simmer to warm through before serving. Check the seasoning and add salt and pepper as needed.

Just before serving your soup, make the crispy lentils. Mix the miso paste with 2 tablespoons of water in a small bowl.

Heat the oil in a large frying pan/skillet over a medium-high heat. Add the cooked lentils and fry for 5–6 minutes, stirring only once or twice, until crispy. Pour in the miso mixture and cook for 30–60 seconds, stirring continuously until the liquid is absorbed. Remove from the heat. Top bowls of soup with the lentils, a drizzle of olive oil and some dukkah to serve.

miso mushroom soup

Mushrooms bring umami and a meaty texture to plant-based dishes, and when paired with miso they create an extra-flavourful broth. I use shiitakes here, but you can play around with different types of mushrooms. Oyster mushrooms and little enoki are great to add to the soup or you could try a mixture of dried mushrooms for the broth.

For the courgette/zucchini noodles, I've used a spiralizer, a vegetable peeler and a julienne peeler, all with good results. If using a spiralizer, break up your noodles, so they're no more than 25 cm/10 inches long, otherwise you can end up with noodles that are too long. If using a vegetable peeler, lay your courgette/zucchini on a cutting board and use the peeler going away from you, from the top end of the courgette/zucchini to the bottom. Continue around the courgette/ zucchini, until you've reached the centre seeds. You should end up with thin strips of courgette/zucchini – or zoodles.

Alternatively, you can replace the courgette/zucchini noodles with cooked soba noodles or similar.

6 dried shiitake mushrooms
4 garlic cloves, chopped in half, skins left on
5-cm/2-inch piece of fresh ginger, roughly chopped
4 tablespoons white or yellow miso paste
1–2 tablespoons tamari or soy sauce
1 tablespoon olive or avocado oil
100 g/3½ oz. fresh shiitake mushrooms, stems removed and thinly sliced into 1.5-cm/½-inch thick pieces
1 small bunch of Tuscan kale, stems removed and thinly sliced into ribbons
2 courgettes/zucchini, spiralized or peeled into noodles
2 large spring onions/ green onions, thinly sliced

SERVES 3-4

Put the dried shiitake mushrooms, garlic and ginger in a large saucepan with a lid. Add 1.5 l/ 6 cups of water, then bring to a boil. Cover, reduce the heat and simmer for 45 minutes. (You can do this a day ahead and place in the fridge.)

Remove the mushrooms, garlic and ginger with a slotted spoon and discard, saving the broth. Bring the broth to a simmer again in a saucepan. Combine the miso with 4 tablespoons of water and whisk together. Add the miso mixture to the broth, then add the tamari 1 slowly, tasting for saltiness. Keep warm or reheat when needed.

In a frying pan/skillet, heat the oil over a medium-high heat. Add the fresh mushrooms and cook, stirring, for 3–4 minutes until golden. Remove from the pan and set aside. Add the kale to the pan and toss for 1–2 minutes until wilted.

To serve, make sure your broth is hot (but not boiling). Place courgette/zucchini noodles, kale and mushrooms in bowls. Ladle over the broth and sprinkle with the spring onions/green onions.

butternut squash & black bean chilli

Cubes of butternut squash and black beans make this chilli hearty and satisfying. I'll make this on a Sunday afternoon to eat throughout the week. The flavours deepen when it has time to sit, so it tastes even better the second or third time around.

I serve it with some diced avocado or guacamole, plain Greek yogurt with a little garlic grated in (instead of sour cream), chopped large spring onions/green onions and/or corn chips.

avocado or olive oil, for frying
1 onion, diced
375 g/3 cups peeled butternut squash, cut into small 1.5-cm/ ½-inch cubes
2 tablespoons tomato purée/paste
1 large garlic clove, finely chopped
3 teaspoons ground cumin
2 teaspoons smoked paprika
¼ teaspoon ground cinnamon
¼ teaspoon cayenne pepper
1 x 400-g/14-oz. can crushed or chopped tomatoes in juices
2 x 400-g/14-oz. cans black beans in their liquid (I use the low sodium version)
salt, to taste

TO SERVE (OPTIONAL)
diced avocado or Guacamole (page 104)
Greek yogurt or sour cream
chopped large spring onions/green onions
corn chips

SERVES 4-6

In a large saucepan with a lid, heat enough oil to cover the base of the pan over a medium heat.

Add the onion, season with salt and cook for about 5 minutes until translucent. Add the butternut squash and cook, stirring occasionally, for 5 minutes.

Add the tomato purée/paste and stir. Cook for 1 minute. Add the garlic, cumin, paprika, cinnamon and cayenne pepper and cook for 1 minute more. Pour in the tomatoes and black beans along with the liquid from the cans. Season with salt and reduce the heat to medium-low.

Cook covered for about 30 minutes, stirring occasionally, until the butternut is tender. You may need to add 120 ml/½ cup or more water, if the chilli becomes too dry or thick for your liking. Serve with desired toppings.

moroccan-spiced lentil stew

This richly spiced tomato-based stew is easy enough to put together on a weeknight and leftovers make a great lunch the next day. I like serving this with warm pita bread.

FOR THE LENTILS
160 g/¾ cup dried black or French/du Puy lentils, soaked for an hour or overnight and drained

FOR THE STEW
olive oil, for frying
1 small red onion, finely diced
1 yellow (bell) pepper, deseeded and finely diced
2 tablespoons tomato purée/paste
2 teaspoons sweet smoked paprika
1 teaspoon ground cumin
½ teaspoon ground coriander

2 garlic cloves, finely chopped
2 x 400-g/14-oz. cans crushed or chopped tomatoes in juice
pinch of saffron threads (optional)
1 large handful of fresh baby spinach, roughly chopped
1 tablespoon harissa
1 tablespoon honey
salt, to taste
freshly chopped parsley or coriander/cilantro, to serve
toasted bread, flatbread or pita, to serve

SERVES 4-5

Put the lentils in a medium saucepan with 710 ml/3 cups of water and a pinch of salt. Bring to a boil, then reduce the heat to medium-low, cover with a lid and cook for about 18–20 minutes. You want them al dente with a little bit of bite. When cooked, drain the lentils in a colander.

Meanwhile, heat a thin layer of oil in a large frying pan/skillet with high sides and a lid or in a dutch oven over a medium heat. Add the onion and (bell) pepper, season with salt and sauté for 4–6 minutes until the onion is translucent.

Stir in the tomato purée/paste and cook for 1 minute. Add the spices and garlic and cook for 30 seconds more. Stir in the tomatoes and saffron (if using). Cover with a lid and simmer over a medium-low heat for 15 minutes.

Add the cooked and drained lentils to the tomato mixture and cook, uncovered, for another 10 minutes, until the liquid has slightly reduced.

Stir in the spinach and let it wilt. Remove from the heat and stir in the harissa and honey. Serve warm scattered with freshly chopped herbs and pita bread to mop up the sauce.

red lentil dahl

This is a perfect store cupboard meal. A combination of lentils, canned tomatoes and a bunch of spices from your arsenal, this is the type of comforting stew you can throw together on a cold afternoon or evening when you really can't be bothered to leave the house.

You can add any greens you like including frozen spinach – no need to get fancy with this one. This is also great with cubes of sweet potato tossed in when you add the carrots.

olive oil, coconut oil or ghee, for frying
2 onions, finely sliced
3 garlic cloves, finely chopped
2.5-cm/1-inch piece of fresh ginger, grated
2 teaspoons ground cumin
1 teaspoon ground turmeric
1 teaspoon ground coriander
½ teaspoon garam masala
¼ teaspoon cayenne pepper
1 x 400-g/14-oz. can chopped tomatoes

270 g/1½ cups dried red lentils
2 carrots, finely diced
120 g/2 cups kale, shredded
salt and freshly ground black pepper, to taste

TO SERVE
steamed rice
pinch of chilli flakes/hot red pepper flakes
freshly chopped coriander/ cilantro
Greek yogurt or coconut cream

SERVES 4–6

Heat enough oil or ghee to thinly coat the base of a large saucepan over a medium-high heat. Add the onions, season to taste with salt and cook for about 10–12 minutes, stirring occasionally, until they begin to caramelize. Add a splash of water if the pan gets too dry.

Add the garlic and ginger and cook for another minute. Stir in the spices and cook for 1 more minute. Add the tomatoes and cook until bubbling again, then add 950 ml/4 cups of water and the lentils. Cover with a lid and bring to a boil.

Add the carrots, cover, and simmer for about 20–30 minutes until the lentils are starting to break down and the carrots are tender. Stir in some black pepper and the kale.

Turn off the heat, leave the pan covered and allow to stand for 15 minutes before serving with rice, chilli flakes/hot red pepper flakes, coriander/ cilantro and a drizzle of yogurt or coconut cream.

sweet potato & white bean stew

White beans lend a creaminess to this stew which, when combined with sweet potato, sage and rosemary, feels like the food version of a cosy sweater. I'm all for canned beans – especially in a pinch – but I really notice a better quality when I cook my own white beans from dried. That said, you can definitely make this stew with canned white beans, so skip step one in the method below if you do.

170 g/1 cup dried white
  beans (or 270 g/
  2 cups cooked
  white beans)
few sprigs of mixed
  fresh herbs (optional)
1 tablespoon olive oil
1 onion, finely diced
3 garlic cloves, finely
  chopped
1 large sweet potato,
  peeled and cut into
  1.5-cm/½-inch cubes

2 carrots, diced
1 tablespoon freshly
  chopped rosemary
  leaves
3 freshly chopped sage
  leaves
950 ml/4 cups
  vegetable stock/
  broth
sea salt and freshly
  ground black pepper,
  to taste
roughly chopped fresh
  parsley, to garnish

SERVES 4-5

If using dried white beans, soak them overnight in cold water for at least 8 hours or longer. When you're ready to cook them, drain off the soaking liquid and discard, then put the beans in a medium saucepan and cover with fresh water.

Bring to a boil, adding a pinch of salt and any fresh herbs you have lying around (a few thyme sprigs, sage leaves, parsley stems, etc.). Simmer for about 30–40 minutes, or until tender. The cooking time will depend on your beans, how long they were soaked for and how old they are. Drain the beans and set aside.

In a large saucepan, heat the olive oil over a medium heat. Add the onion and cook, stirring occasionally, for about 5 minutes, until softened. Add the garlic and cook for 1 minute more. Stir in the sweet potato, carrots, rosemary and sage. Season well with salt and cook for another 2–3 minutes until the herbs are fragrant.

Add the cooked and drained white beans and the vegetable stock/broth and bring everything to a boil. Simmer over a medium-low heat, covered with a lid for 20 minutes until the sweet potato has softened. Uncover, stir and simmer for a final 5 minutes. Crush a few white beans against the side of the pot with a wooden spoon to release their starch and thicken the stew. Spoon the stew into bowls and garnish with chopped parsley and freshly ground black pepper to serve.

Thai vegetable curry

This is my weeknight takeout alternative. A coconut-based and spice-flecked curry that's so packed with good vegetables, no one will miss the meat. We're avoiding the standard wimpy carrot discs in favour of heartier winter squash, (bell) peppers, broccoli and edamame beans (or green peas) for a curry that really celebrates vegetables.

It's easy, full of colour and you can make it ahead and reheat over a low heat when you're ready to eat.

coconut or avocado oil, for frying
1 onion, finely diced
1 yellow (bell) pepper, deseeded and chopped into thin strips
1 tablespoon grated fresh ginger
1 tablespoon freshly chopped coriander/cilantro stems (leaves reserved for serving)
2 tablespoons red Thai curry paste, or more to taste
235 ml/1 cup vegetable stock/broth
250 g/2 cups butternut squash or kabocha pumpkin, peeled and cut into 1.5-cm/½-inch chunks
1 x 400-g/14-oz. can coconut milk (I use full fat)
1 tablespoon tamari
1 crown of broccoli, cut into small florets
130 g/1 cup frozen shelled edamame beans or green peas, thawed
salt, to taste
cooked brown rice or quinoa, to serve (optional)

SERVES 4

Heat a thin layer of oil in a large saucepan over a medium-high heat. Add the onion, (bell) pepper and a pinch of salt and cook for 5 minutes, stirring occasionally.

Add the ginger, coriander/cilantro stems and curry paste and cook, stirring, for 1 minute. Add the vegetable stock/broth and the butternut squash or pumpkin and stir to combine. Reduce the heat to medium, cover with a lid and cook for 7–8 minutes.

Stir in the coconut milk, tamari, broccoli and edamame beans or peas, cover with a lid and bring to a boil. Reduce the heat and simmer for another 3–5 minutes until the butternut squash and broccoli are tender and easily pierced with a fork. Remove from the heat and allow to stand for 5 minutes uncovered.

Taste for seasoning, adding more salt if needed, and serve warm over cooked rice or quinoa (if desired) and top with fresh coriander/cilantro leaves to serve.

BIG BOWLS

A plant-eater's favourite way to eat. More than a salad, but still requiring a high-sided dish to contain them, these combos of grains, veggies, legumes, sauces and more are what I eat most often for lunches and dinners.

sweet potato noodle bowl
with almond butter-ginger sauce

Sweet potato noodles are one of my favourite food discoveries. I love a simple baked sweet potato loaded with toppings for an easy and colourful dinner, and sweet potato noodles are that idea completely reimagined.

The almond butter sauce is a riff on a rich peanut satay sauce, packed with garlic and ginger for Thai-inspired flavour. The garnishes of lime and mint really take this dish to the next level in terms of freshness and taste, but coriander/cilantro would be great here, too.

A vegetable spiralizer works really well for making lovely long strands of sweet potato quickly, but you can also use a julienne peeler or even pre-cut veggie noodles from a grocery store.

1 small crown of broccoli, sliced into small florets

2 teaspoons avocado or olive oil

2 small or 1 large sweet potato, peeled and spiralized or peeled into noodles

1 tablespoon tamari

1 garlic clove, finely chopped

2 large spring onions/ green onions, sliced

salt, to taste

freshly chopped mint leaves and lime wedges, to garnish

FOR THE ALMOND BUTTER SAUCE

3 tablespoons tamari

2 tablespoons almond butter

1 tablespoon rice vinegar

1 tablespoon grated fresh ginger

1 garlic clove, finely chopped

1 teaspoon chilli/chili paste

SERVES 2

To make the almond butter sauce, combine the ingredients along with a splash of water in a tall jar and blend with a stick blender or whisk in a bowl until everything is well combined (make sure your ginger and garlic are very finely chopped if whisking). Set aside until needed.

Put the broccoli in a bowl and pour over boiling water to cover. Leave to stand for about 5 minutes, then drain.

Meanwhile, heat the oil in a large saucepan over a medium-high heat. Add the sweet potato noodles, a pinch of salt and about a tablespoon of water and stir. Cover and cook for about 3–4 minutes, until slightly tender.

Add the broccoli, tamari, garlic and large spring onions/green onions and cook for another 2–3 minutes, stirring frequently. Add more water (a spoonful at a time) if you notice the noodles sticking to the pan. Once the noodles are softened slightly and the garlic is fragrant, remove from the heat.

Drizzle with a few spoons of almond butter sauce and stir to coat. Divide into two bowls and top with mint leaves, lime wedges and extra sauce.

mezze bowl

Lots of texture, flavours and freshness make this recipe one you'll want to share. Any of the tahini dressings from the basics chapter would be nice here, or serve with Garlic Greens and Hummus, along with a side of pita.

5–7 carrots, sliced diagonally into ovals
1 tablespoon olive oil, plus extra to serve
1 teaspoon red wine vinegar
1 teaspoon ground cumin
85 g/½ cup dried quinoa
large handful of freshly chopped mint leaves
large handful of freshly chopped parsley
seeds from ½ pomegranate
¼ cucumber, cut into small pieces
freshly squeezed juice of half a lemon
salt

FOR THE BOWL TOPPINGS (OPTIONAL)
Garlic Greens (page 21)
warm pita
Garlic Yogurt Dip (page 17)
Hummus (page 144)
Tahini-harissa Dressing (page 13)

SERVES 2-3

Preheat the oven to 200°C (400°F) Gas 6.

Toss the carrots with the olive oil, vinegar, cumin and a pinch of salt. Spread out on a baking tray and roast in the preheated oven for about 30 minutes (rotating the tray at the 15 minute mark).

Meanwhile, in a small saucepan, combine the quinoa with 235 ml/1 cup of water. Bring to a boil, add a pinch of salt and reduce to a simmer. Cover with a lid and simmer for about 15 minutes, or until all the liquid is absorbed. Remove from the heat and keep covered for about 10 minutes. Fluff with a fork and allow to cool.

In a bowl, combine the cooled quinoa with the chopped herbs, pomegranate seeds, cucumber, lemon juice and a drizzle of oil and toss to mix.

Divide the quinoa into bowls. Add the roasted carrots and any extra toppings you like.

green kitchari bowl

Kitchari has intrigued me since I first learned about it a few years ago. It's a simple concept – a combination of lentils or split peas, rice and spices – but the result is something wholesome and deeply comforting, kind of like an Indian-spiced risotto.

Originating in South Asia, in the traditional healing concept of ayurveda, it's often used as a cleansing meal to healthily balance the three bodily doshas.

I've included fenugreek in this recipe, as its purported health benefits (including digestive support) add to the healing properties in this dish, plus it smells delicious. However, if it's too hard to get your hands on feel free to skip it.

180 g/1 cup dried yellow split peas or lentils
90 g/½ cup long grain brown or jasmine rice
2–3 tablespoons ghee or coconut oil
1 tablespoon grated fresh ginger
2 teaspoons ground cumin
1 teaspoon ground coriander
1 teaspoon fennel seeds
1 teaspoon ground fenugreek
1 teaspoon ground turmeric

1.2 litres/5 cups water or vegetable stock/broth
1 crown broccoli, cut up very small into an almost rice-like texture
1 medium courgette/zucchini, trimmed and coarsely grated
60 g/1 packed cup baby spinach or baby kale, roughly chopped
salt, to taste
freshly chopped coriander/cilantro, to serve
Garlic Yogurt Dip (optional) (page 17), to serve

SERVES 4-6

Rinse the yellow split peas or lentils and rice in a colander under cold water until the water runs clear.

In a large saucepan over a medium-high heat, heat enough ghee or coconut oil to cover the base of the pan. Add the ginger and cook, stirring, for 30 seconds. Add the spices, season with salt and cook for another 30 seconds, until fragrant.

Add the lentils and rice and stir to coat in the spices. Pour in the water or vegetable stock/broth and bring to a boil.

Reduce the heat to medium-low, cover with a lid and simmer for 35–45 minutes, stirring occasionally until the rice and lentils are tender but not mushy and most of the liquid has been absorbed. (You may need to add a little more liquid if the mixture becomes too dry.)

Stir in the broccoli. Cover and cook for another 4–5 minutes. Stir in the courgette/zucchini and spinach or kale, then remove from the heat and leave to stand for 5 minutes. Serve warm scattered with freshly chopped coriander/cilantro and garlic yogurt dip, if desired.

cumin spiced pumpkin
with cauliflower & chickpeas

Za'atar is a spice blend featuring sumac, a herb with bright, lemon-like qualities. If you you find yourself reaching for the same spices every time you cook, give this new blend a try. The za'atar recipe below makes more than you need for this recipe, so you'll have a chance to try it a few other ways. Use as a sprinkle to liven up roasted vegetables, dressings and dips.

FOR THE ZA'ATAR

1 tablespoon fresh thyme leaves (or 2 teaspoons dried thyme)
1 tablespoon sumac
1 tablespoon ground cumin
1 tablespoon sesame seeds
1 teaspoon salt
1 teaspoon freshly ground black pepper

FOR THE BOWLS

250 g/2 cups peeled and deseeded pumpkin or winter squash, chopped into 2.5-cm/1-inch cubes (butternut or kabocha are great)
1 small head or ½ large head of cauliflower, chopped into small florets
140 g/1 cup cooked chickpeas, drained, rinsed and dried
2 tablespoons olive oil
1 tablespoon Za'atar

3 big handfuls of rocket/arugula
5 radicchio leaves, finely sliced into ribbons
4 pitted dates or figs, sliced
20 fresh mint leaves, torn or roughly chopped
25 g/¼ cup pistachios, shelled and roughly chopped

FOR THE HONEY BALSAMIC DRESSING

60 ml/¼ cup extra-virgin olive oil
2 tablespoons aged balsamic vinegar
2 teaspoons Dijon mustard
1 teaspoon honey or maple syrup
salt, to taste

SERVES 2-3

Preheat the oven to 220°C (425°F) Gas 7.

Combine the za'atar ingredients in a small jar with a lid and shake together.

In a large bowl, toss the pumpkin, cauliflower and chickpeas with the oil until well coated. Add the za'atar and toss again to coat in the spices. Spread out on two baking trays and roast in the preheated oven for 30–35 minutes until golden (rotating the tray at the 15 minute mark).

While the vegetables are cooking, combine the dressing ingredients with 1 tablespoon of water in a jar with a lid and shake until everything is well combined. Adjust the seasoning to taste.

When the vegetables are cooked, toss the rocket/arugula and radicchio with a two spoonfuls of dressing (a little goes a long way) and divide between bowls.

Add the roasted vegetables and chickpeas, dates or figs, mint and pistachios. Drizzle with more dressing, if desired.

aglio e olio quinoa bowl

Garlic and olive oil (aglio e olio) is one of the simplest yet most gratifying pasta dishes. I like to give my weeknight quinoa the pasta treatment for a real flavour boost.

170 g/1 cup quinoa, rinsed
¼ teaspoon salt
2 tablespoons olive oil, plus more as needed
5 garlic cloves, finely chopped
¼ teaspoon chilli flakes/hot red pepper flakes
1 teaspoon nutritional yeast (optional)

salt and freshly ground black pepper, to taste

TO SERVE
Pan-grilled Broccoli (page 22)
2–4 tablespoons toasted pine nuts
freshly grated pecorino or Parmesan (optional)

SERVES 2-3

Combine the quinoa with 475 ml/2 cups of water and the salt in a medium saucepan. Bring to a boil, then cover and reduce the heat to medium-low. Cook for 15–20 minutes until all the liquid has been absorbed. Remove from the heat, fluff with a fork and let stand, covered, for 10 minutes.

In a large saucepan or frying pan/skillet with high sides, combine the olive oil and garlic. Heat over a medium-low heat until the garlic is sizzling. Cook, stirring, for 1–2 minutes until fragrant and turning slightly golden. Add the chilli flakes/hot red pepper flakes, then the cooked quinoa and nutritional yeast (if using) and stir to combine. Cook for 1 minute, stirring constantly. Season to taste with salt and pepper and divide between bowls. To serve, top with the broccoli, toasted pine nuts and a sprinkle of cheese (if using).

cblt salad bowl
with avocado & chickpeas

Coconut Bacon. Lettuce. Tomato. Oh, and avocado, of course. This simple salad uses flaked coconut and oven-baked chickpeas to capture the flavour and crunch of bacon. Sweet honey mustard brings the whole thing together for a bowl that's fresh and fun.

Crispy Chickpeas (page 9)
Coconut Bacon Bits (page 21)
1 tablespoon Honey Mustard Dressing (page 11), plus extra to serve
1 head of Cos/romaine lettuce, finely sliced

170 g/1 heaped cup cherry tomatoes, quartered
1 avocado, peeled, pitted and sliced into small pieces

SERVES 2-3

If you haven't made your crispy chickpeas, coconut bacon bits and honey mustard dressing, get to work on those first.

Gather the rest of the salad ingredients. In a large bowl, combine the lettuce with a spoonful of the honey mustard dressing and toss to combine. Fold in the tomatoes and avocado.

Divide into smaller bowls and top with the crispy chickpeas, coconut bacon bits and then drizzle over extra dressing as desired.

bánh mì bowl

This spicy bowl has a few more ingredients than most, but I promise
it's easy to put together and perfect for sharing.

To make your tofu extra crispy, remember to press the water out
of it for at least 5 minutes before using. I like to wrap the drained block
of tofu in paper towels, put it on top of a clean kitchen cloth and place
a heavy book or pan on top for good measure.

**FOR THE QUICK
PICKLED CARROTS**

120 ml/½ cup white
  wine vinegar
120 ml/½ cup room
  temperature water
1 tablespoon coconut
  or cane sugar
1 teaspoon salt
2 large carrots, cut into
  julienne or peeled
  into ribbons

FOR THE RICE

100 g/½ cup sushi rice
salt, to taste

**FOR THE SRIRACHA
CREAM**

100 g/½ cup Greek
  yogurt
1–2 teaspoons sriracha
  hot sauce
2 teaspoons olive oil
1 small or ½ large
  garlic clove, finely
  chopped or grated
salt, to taste

**FOR THE BOWL
TOPPINGS**

150 g/1 cup cucumber,
  quartered and cut
  into 1.5-cm/½-inch
  pieces
3 radishes, very thinly
  sliced
1 jalapeño, thinly sliced
large handful of fresh
  coriander/cilantro
  leaves
large handful of fresh
  mint leaves, stems
  removed
1 avocado, peeled,
  pitted and sliced
Spicy Tofu (page 10)
fresh lime wedges,
  to serve

SERVES 3-4

For the quick pickled carrots, combine the vinegar,
water, sugar and salt in a medium mixing bowl
and stir to dissolve the sugar and salt. Add the
carrots and toss to coat in the pickling liquid.
Leave to stand for at least 20 minutes.

Cook the sushi rice in 235 ml/1 cup of boiling
water according to the package instructions,
until tender and sticky. Season to taste with salt.

Meanwhile, to make the sriracha cream, whisk
together the ingredients in a small bowl and
season to taste with salt.

Make sure your bowl toppings are all prepped
and ready to go. Assemble your bowls with a
portion of rice at the base, followed by the quick
pickled carrots (drained from the pickling juices).

Pile the bowls with the cucumber, radishes,
jalapeño, fresh herbs, avocado and spicy tofu.
Serve with a drizzle of the sriracha cream and
lime wedges for squeezing over.

plantain bowl
with lime & coriander/cilantro dressing

Pan-fried plantains are a lovely starchy addition to a dish as an alternative to potatoes or sweet potatoes. I look for plantains on the green side, as they're less sweet and hold their shape well.

For a slightly richer bowl, serve with the Garlic Yogurt Dip (page 17) or the Creamy Chipotle Dip (page 17).

avocado oil, for frying
1 plantain, peeled and
    sliced into 1.5-cm/
    ½-inch thick rounds
120–180 g/2–3 cups red
    cabbage or kale (or
    a combination of the
    two), very thinly
    sliced
200 g/1 cup barbecue
    Black Beans (page 9)
60 g/½ cup cherry
    tomatoes, sliced
1 avocado, peeled,
    pitted and cut into
    bite-sized chunks
salt, to taste

**FOR THE LIME &
CORIANDER/CILANTRO
DRESSING**
30 g/1 cup coriander/
    cilantro leaves
½ garlic clove
4 tablespoons olive oil
2 tablespoons fresh
    lime juice (about half
    a lime)
1 tablespoon finely
    chopped shallot

SERVES 2

In a large frying pan/skillet, heat enough oil to just cover the base over a medium heat. Add the plantain slices (they need space to cook so you may need to fry them in batches depending on the size of your pan). Season with salt and fry for about 2–3 minutes, then flip and cook for another 2 minutes or until slightly browned and golden. Transfer to paper towels to blot any excess oil and repeat with the remaining plantain slices.

To make the dressing, add the ingredients along with 1 tablespoon of water to a food processor or use a jar and stick blender. Blend until you get a herb-flecked dressing without any large leaves of coriander/cilantro. Or, you can finely chop the herbs and garlic and whisk everything together by hand until well combined. Season with salt.

Toss the cabbage or kale with a few spoonfuls of green dressing, adding more as needed. If you're using kale, feel free to massage the dressing into the kale leaves with your hands to soften them.

Assemble the bowls with a base of red cabbage and/or kale, top with barbecue black beans, the fried plantain, cherry tomatoes and the avocado chunks. Add more green dressing, or a creamy dip or sauce of your choice, if desired.

winter vegetable bowl

Winter can be rough on us veggie lovers, when farm fresh tomatoes and juicy stone fruit seem another world away. Here's a bowl that celebrates cold weather produce and perks it up with a tasty lemon and olive chermoula and crunchy toasted walnuts.

130 g/¾ cup wild rice
1 acorn squash, sliced in half and seeds removed, then sliced into thin half-moons
1 red onion, cut into 1.5-cm/½-inch wedges
1–2 tablespoons avocado or olive oil
300 g/3 cups Brussels sprouts, woody bases and outer leaves removed, then thinly sliced (so you get ribbons of Brussels sprouts leaves)

2 big handfuls of baby rocket/arugula or spinach
salt and freshly ground black pepper, to taste
Chermoula (page 14), to serve
50 g/⅓ cup toasted walnuts, roughly chopped, to serve

a baking tray, oiled

SERVES 3-4

Preheat the oven to 220°C (425°F) Gas 7.

In a medium saucepan, combine the wild rice with 350 ml/1½ cups of water. Cover with a lid and bring to a boil. Add a pinch of salt, reduce the heat to medium-low and simmer for about 40 minutes, or according to the package instructions, until the rice is cooked.

Meanwhile, arrange the squash and onion on the prepared baking tray. Roast in the preheated oven for about 25–30 minutes, rotating the tray and flipping the veg half-way through.

Meanwhile, heat the oil in a large saucepan or a frying pan/skillet with high sides over a medium-high heat. Add the shredded Brussels sprouts and sprinkle with a good pinch of salt. Cook, stirring a few times, for about 5 minutes until the sprouts are softened; they should be mostly bright green but golden in places. Stir in the rocket/arugula or spinach and remove from the heat. Taste and add salt and pepper as desired.

To assemble the bowls, start with a scoop of rice and top with lots of Brussels sprouts, roasted squash and red onion. Add a generous drizzle of chermoula and walnuts to finish.

coconut brown rice bowl
with jerk spice roasted vegetables

Warming jerk spices, creamy coconut rice and bright lime juice make for a low-key tropical bowl for all seasons.

You can swap the courgette/zucchini and asparagus for other vegetables, if you like (though roasting times will vary). Roasted carrots, (bell) pepper and winter squash are all great here, too.

FOR THE COCONUT BROWN RICE

100 g/½ cup brown rice

75 ml/⅓ cup coconut milk

pinch of salt

FOR THE JERK SPICE MIX (MAKES ABOUT 25 G/¼ CUP)

1 teaspoon ground allspice

1 teaspoon curry powder

1 teaspoon onion powder

½ teaspoon garlic powder

½ teaspoon cayenne pepper

¼ teaspoon ground ginger

¼ teaspoon ground nutmeg

¼ teaspoon freshly ground black pepper

1 teaspoon salt

FOR THE VEGETABLES

2 courgettes/zucchini or yellow summer squash, cut diagonally into 1.5-cm/½-inch thick ovals

1–2 tablespoons olive oil

1 bunch of asparagus, woody ends snapped off and cut into bite-sized pieces

salt and freshly ground black pepper

TO SERVE

1 spring onion/scallion, finely chopped

1 avocado, peeled, pitted and cut into bite-sized pieces

toasted pumpkin seeds/pepitas or Crispy Chickpeas (page 9)

lime wedges

SERVES 2-3

Combine the rice, coconut milk and 235 ml/1 cup of water in a saucepan over a medium-high heat. Cover with a lid and bring to a boil. Add the salt, then reduce the heat to medium-low and simmer, covered, for about 40–45 minutes until the rice is cooked and creamy and the liquid has been absorbed.

Meanwhile, combine all the jerk spice mix ingredients in a small jar with a lid and shake until blended together.

Preheat the oven to 200°C (400°F) Gas 6.

In a large bowl, mix together the courgettes/zucchini with enough olive oil to coat and about 2 teaspoons of the jerk spice mix. Toss well to coat the courgettes/zucchini in the spice. Spread the courgettes/zucchini out on a baking tray, being careful not to crowd them. Repeat by tossing the asparagus in the oil and jerk spice mix and spread out on a separate baking tray.

Roast the vegetables in the preheated oven for about 15–20 minutes, turning halfway through, until golden. Taste and adjust the seasoning with salt and pepper, if needed.

Assemble the bowls starting with a portion of coconut rice, then the roasted spiced vegetables, spring onion/scallion, avocado and toasted pumpkin seeds/pepitas or crispy chickpeas. Serve with lime wedges for squeezing over.

buffalo cauliflower & chickpea bowl
with kale & tahini ranch dressing

I grew up on chicken wings. The spicy, hot buffalo-style ones that come with a side of blue cheese sauce, carrot and celery sticks. This bar food was strangely one of my favourite meals from ages five to eight. My dad even talked about my love of buffalo wings in his speech at my wedding, which was both embarrassing and very fitting.

Now I often eat buffalo-style vegetables, because I like the best of both worlds – hearty roasted vegetables and messy, spicy sauces. Any hot sauce will work here – I have a nostalgic affinity for Frank's but Tessemae's makes a great all-natural buffalo version.

FOR THE CAULIFLOWER
- 1 small-medium sized head of cauliflower, chopped into florets
- 1 tablespoon olive oil
- 3 tablespoons hot sauce
- salt, to taste

FOR THE CHICKPEAS
- 1 tablespoon avocado or olive oil
- 1 x 400-g/14-oz. can chickpeas, drained and rinsed
- ¼ teaspoon garlic powder
- 2 tablespoons hot sauce

FOR THE SALAD
- 1 bunch of Tuscan kale, stems removed and shredded
- 2 tablespoons Tahini-ranch Dressing (page 13), plus extra to serve
- 1 large carrot, peeled into ribbons
- ½ small red onion, very thinly sliced into half-moons

SERVES 2-4

Preheat the oven to 220°C (425°F) Gas 7.

In a large bowl, combine the cauliflower with the oil and 1 tablespoon of the hot sauce. Season with salt and mix together until the cauliflower is well coated. Spread out on a baking tray and roast in the preheated oven for 20 minutes. Take out and toss with the remaining 2 tablespoons of hot sauce. Return to the oven for 5–10 minutes until the cauliflower is lightly browned at the edges.

To make the chickpeas, heat the oil in a large frying pan/skillet over a medium-high heat, then add the chickpeas and garlic powder and season with salt. Cook for 3 minutes, tossing regularly. Stir in 1 tablespoon of the hot sauce and cook, stirring, for 2–3 minutes, until the chickpeas are starting to brown. Remove from the heat and stir in the remaining 1 tablespoon of hot sauce.

Combine the kale with 1–2 tablespoons of tahini ranch dressing in a large bowl. Massage into the kale for 2 minutes until it begins to soften a little. Toss in the carrot and red onion and mix until everything is well coated in the dressing. Divide the salad into bowls and top with the cauliflower, chickpeas and extra tahini ranch dressing.

nicoise-ish salad bowl

I think I ate a Salade Nicoise as soon as I arrived in Paris for the first time. It wasn't an earth-shattering salad, but certain elements like the briny olives, creamy boiled potatoes, and a spot-on vinaigrette left an impression on me.

This is no wimpy side salad, this is a big, substantial lunch salad that will power you through an afternoon of work or play.

150 g/¾ cup dried black or French/du Puy lentils, soaked for an hour or overnight and drained
1 small bunch of radishes (about 6– 8), sliced in half lengthwise
450 g/1 lb. green beans, trimmed
225 g/8 oz. small baby potatoes
1 tablespoon avocado or olive oil
1 teaspoon fresh thyme leaves
2 teaspoons capers, drained
4 large handfuls of baby rocket/arugula, roughly chopped
170 g/1 cup grape tomatoes, chopped
¼–⅓ cup olives, pitted and sliced (I like to use nicoise, nyon or Kalamata)
salt, to taste

FOR THE DRESSING
2 teaspoons Dijon mustard
2 teaspoons red wine vinegar
4 tablespoons olive oil
2 tablespoons very finely chopped shallot
salt and freshly ground black pepper, to taste

2 baking trays, oiled

SERVES 2-4

First, cook the lentils in a medium saucepan with 710 ml/3 cups of water and a pinch of salt. Bring to a boil, cover with a lid and simmer for about 18–20 minutes. You want them al dente with a little bit of bite. Drain the lentils well, keeping them in the colander for at least 10 minutes to make sure they are fairly dry.

Preheat the oven to 200°C (400°F) Gas 6.

Arrange the radishes on one of the prepared baking trays and the green beans on the other. Roast the radishes in the preheated oven for 25 minutes and the green beans for 15–20 minutes.

Meanwhile, fill a medium saucepan half full with water and bring to a boil. Add a big pinch of salt and the potatoes and boil for about 10–12 minutes until the potatoes are easily pierced with a fork. Drain and run the potatoes under cold water. When cool enough to handle, slice in half.

Heat the oil in a large frying pan/skillet over a medium-high heat. Add the cooked and drained lentils and the thyme. Season with salt and cook for 5–6 minutes, stirring only once or twice, until crispy. Stir in the capers and cook for 1 minute, then remove from the heat.

Whisk together all the dressing ingredients with 2 tablespoons of water in a bowl until combined.

Assemble the salad bowls by tossing the rocket/arugula with a spoonful or two of dressing and dividing between the bowls. Top with the green beans, potatoes, tomatoes, radishes, crispy lentils and olives. Drizzle over extra dressing to serve.

soy & ginger delicata winter squash bowl

Delicata squash is kind of the best- it looks fancy, you don't have to peel it and it has a subtle nuttiness that goes well with so many different flavours. I recommend roasting a big batch ahead of time and using some in this dish.

If you can't get your hands on delicata, you can use whatever roasted vegetables you have (broccoli, butternut or peppers would all be nice). Serve with a drizzle of sriracha or chilli paste for a spicier bowl.

1 delicata squash, cut in half lengthwise, deseeded and sliced into half-moons

175 g/6 oz. soba noodles

1 tablespoon olive or avocado oil

2.5-cm/1-inch piece of fresh ginger, finely grated

2 garlic cloves, finely chopped

50 g/2 cups kale, stems removed and shredded

3 tablespoons tamari or soy sauce

1 tablespoon maple syrup or honey

2 large spring onions/ green onions, thinly sliced, to serve

toasted sesame seeds, to serve (optional)

a baking tray, oiled

SERVES 2-3

Preheat the oven to 220°C (425°F) Gas 7.

Arrange the squash on the prepared baking tray so that each piece has plenty of room. Roast in the preheated oven for 20–25 minutes, until golden, flipping with a spatula halfway through.

Meanwhile, cook the soba noodles in boiling water following the package instructions (I cook mine for 6 minutes, but the cooking time will vary according to the type of noodle). Drain and rinse under cold water while in the colander.

In a large frying pan/skillet, heat the oil over a medium-high heat. Add the ginger and garlic and cook, stirring, for 1 minute. Add the kale and cook for about 2–3 minutes until wilted.

Add the tamari or soy and maple syrup or honey and stir vigorously to combine. Add the noodles and squash and stir gently to coat everything.

Portion into bowls and serve with large spring onions/green onions and toasted sesame seeds.

autumn butternut squash noodle bowl

Usher in autumn/fall with this tangle of butternut noodles. It's still light enough for Indian summer temperatures, but it's filled with all those earthy flavours that we're ready for come September.

Sage and garlic are natural flavour buddies for butternut squash, and this dish plays on that classic pasta combination by making the squash the noodles instead of just an add-in.

And best of all, it all comes together quick enough for a weeknight dinner. Vegetarians and omnivores might like a grating of Parmesan and/or a fried egg on top, too.

1 large butternut squash, the top handle part only, peeled*
olive oil for frying, plus extra for serving
140 g/2 cups mushrooms (I used cremini), sliced
3 garlic cloves, finely chopped
10 fresh sage leaves, finely chopped
salt and freshly ground black pepper, to taste
3 tablespoons roughly chopped toasted walnuts, to serve

SERVES 2

Make the butternut noodles by using a spiralizer or a julienne peeler. You should get a big pile of noodles if you're using a large-ish squash. If you're using a spiralizer, remember to break up the noodles so they aren't extra long.

Heat a thin layer of olive oil in a large, high-sided frying pan/skillet over a medium-high heat. Add the mushrooms, half of the garlic, and a good pinch of salt. Cook, stirring only a couple of times, for about 5–6 minutes, until softened and golden. Stir in a pinch of the chopped sage leaves (leaving most of them for later). Remove the mushrooms from the pan and set aside.

Heat another thin layer of olive oil over a medium-high heat. Add the butternut noodles, remaining garlic and another couple of pinches of salt and stir. Cook for about 2 minutes, stirring once or twice.

Add a little splash (just a tablespoon or two) of water and cover the pan. Cook for another 3–4 minutes, until the butternut is tender.

Stir in the remaining sage and the mushrooms until everything is well combined. Taste for seasoning, adding more salt if needed and a crack of black pepper.

Serve divided between two bowls and topped with toasted walnuts and another drizzle of olive oil.

*Deseed the bottom hollowed-out part, cut into pieces, and roast at 220°C (425°F) Gas 7 for about 30 minutes. Add to salads, bowls or a savoury porridge.

stir fry bowl

Some weeknights require a good stir fry to end things on a simple but satisfying note. If you made a batch of Spicy Tofu (page 10) in advance, this is where you can put leftovers to good use.

100 g/½ cup brown rice (I also like a mixture of wild and brown rice)
pinch of salt
1 tablespoon peeled and very finely chopped fresh ginger
2 garlic cloves, very finely chopped
4 large spring onions/ green onions, thinly sliced
1 bunch of baby broccoli, broccolini or regular broccoli (about 120 g/2 cups), cut into bite-sized pieces

200 g/2 cups mangetout/ snow peas
avocado oil, for frying
1 teaspoon sherry vinegar
2 tablespoons tamari
½ portion of Spicy Tofu (page 10)
sesame seeds, to garnish (optional)

SERVES 2

Combine the rice and 235 ml/1 cup of water in a saucepan over a medium-high heat. Cover with a lid and bring to a boil. Add the pinch of salt, then reduce the heat to medium-low and simmer, covered, for about 35–40 minutes until the rice is tender and the water has been absorbed.

Towards the end of the rice cooking time, mix the ginger, garlic and large spring onions/green onions together in a small bowl. Combine the broccoli and mange tout/snow peas on a plate, ready for frying. Depending on the size of your pan, you may need to divide all the ingredients (including the oil, vinegar and tamari) in half and fry in two batches to avoid overcrowding.

In a large wok or frying pan/skillet, heat a thin layer of oil over a high heat. Add the onion mixture and cook for 5 seconds. Toss in the broccoli and mangetout/snow peas and stir fry for about 5–6 minutes until seared and golden. If you need to re-heat the spicy tofu, add this now to warm through. Add the sherry vinegar and tamari and stir fry for 30–60 seconds. Remove from the pan and transfer to a plate. Repeat the process with the remaining ingredients if needed.

Drain and then divide the hot cooked rice into bowls. Pile the vegetables and spicy tofu on top and serve with a sprinkling of sesame seeds to garnish, if you like.

ENTERTAINING

Delicious plant-centric dishes for sharing with friends. These entertaining ideas are all about offering everyone options for serving themselves, which can include cheese, eggs or a little meat to keep everyone happy – including the host.

TACO PARTY

Tacos are one of the best and easiest ways to feed a big group of hungry people. Stock up on lots of tortillas and corn chips and make a few different fillings and dips so that everyone can mix and match.

My number one rule is: always have more guac. Guests can have it with salsa and chips on arrival and you'll want it as a topping for all your tacos, so it's best to have a stock pile of avocados ready to go.

You can also make most of the main components ahead of time, and when you're ready to eat, simply warm a few things up (including your tortillas) and create an assembly line of fillings. To make it a bigger feast, serve the Vegetable-loaded Nachos (page 149) or Stuffed Poblano Peppers (page 111), too.

This taco party includes:

Barbecue Black Beans (page 9)
5-Seed Slaw (page 22)
Spicy Sweet Potato Filling (recipe right)
Veggie Fajita Filling (recipe right)
Guacamole (recipe right)
Hot Sauce
Tortillas
Corn chips

SERVES 4-6

guacamole

Do you really need a guac recipe? Great guacamole is based on personal preference and this one's mine. Make your guac just before everyone is set to arrive to keep the green vibrant.

4 ripe avocados, peeled and pitted
½ small red onion, finely diced
handful of freshly chopped coriander/cilantro
1 tablespoon finely chopped jalapeño (optional)
freshly squeezed juice of ½ lime
salt, to taste

Scoop the avocado flesh into a medium-sized mixing bowl. Mash the avocados lightly with a fork, leaving the texture a bit chunky.

Stir in the red onion, coriander/cilantro, jalapeño (if using) and lime juice. Season to taste with salt, stir well and then transfer to a fresh, clean bowl to serve.

veggie fajita filling

avocado oil, for frying
225 g/8 oz. baby portobello mushrooms,
  thinly sliced
1 small red onion, cut into wedges
1 red (bell) pepper, deseeded and cut into strips
1 yellow (bell) pepper, deseeded and cut into strips
salt, to taste

Heat enough oil to cover the base of a large frying pan/skillet over a medium-high heat. Add the mushrooms, season with salt and stir. Cook for 3–4 minutes, stirring once or twice, until browned in parts. Transfer to a plate and set aside until needed.

In the same pan, heat another glug of oil over a medium-high heat. Add the onion and (bell) peppers, season with salt and stir. Cover with a lid and cook for 3 minutes.

Remove the lid, stir and cook for another 2–3 minutes, adding a tablespoon or two of water if the mixture is too dry. Cook until the water has evaporated and the onion and (bell) peppers are softened and browned in places. Pile into a dish to serve.

spicy sweet potato filling

2 medium sweet potatoes, peeled
  and chopped into 1.5-cm/½-inch cubes
1 medium red onion, sliced into
  1.5-cm/½-inch wedges
1 tablespoon avocado or olive oil
1 teaspoon ground cumin
¼ teaspoon cayenne pepper
salt, to taste

Preheat the oven to 220°C (425°F) Gas 7.

Combine the sweet potatoes, onion, oil, cumin and cayenne pepper in a medium-sized mixing bowl. Season with salt and toss together.

Spread the sweet potato and red onion mixture onto a baking tray. Bake in the preheated oven for 20–25 minutes (turning halfway through), until golden and tender. Pile into a clean bowl to serve.

chickpea 'tikka' masala

The Indian takeout staple gets a plant-based makeover with chickpeas in a lush tomato-based sauce. Serve with fluffy rice, chopped chilli/chile, fresh herbs and naan breads on the side for a simple and satisfying feast.

coconut oil or ghee,
   for frying
1 onion, finely diced
1 yellow (bell) pepper,
   deseeded and finely
   chopped
2 garlic cloves, finely
   chopped
2 teaspoons garam
   masala
1 teaspoon ground
   cumin
½ teaspoon ground
   turmeric
2 carrots, finely
   chopped
2 x 400-g/14-oz. cans
   of chickpeas, drained
   and rinsed
2 x 400-g/14-oz. cans
   of finely chopped
   tomatoes in juice or
   crushed tomatoes

1 x-400-g/14-oz. can
   coconut milk (I use
   full fat)
¼ teaspoon cayenne
   pepper (optional)
salt, to taste

TO SERVE (OPTIONAL)
cooked brown rice
   or quinoa
naan breads
freshly chopped
   coriander/cilantro
   leaves
freshly chopped
   chilli/chile

SERVES 6

Heat enough coconut oil or ghee to generously coat the bottom of a large saucepan over a medium-high heat.

Add the onion and (bell) pepper and season with salt. Cook, stirring, for about 10 minutes.

Add the garlic and cook for 1 minute. Add the garam masala, cumin and turmeric and cook for another 30 seconds, until fragrant.

Add the carrots, chickpeas and tomatoes. Bring to a boil, then reduce to a simmer and cover with a lid. Simmer for about 15–20 minutes.

Stir in the coconut milk, then simmer for 5 minutes more and remove from the heat. Stir in the cayenne pepper, if using. Let the curry stand, covered with a lid to keep warm, for at least 15 minutes to let the flavours mingle.

Serve over brown rice or quinoa, with naan breads, fresh herbs and chilli/chile, as desired.

stuffed poblano peppers

Stuffed peppers make a great meal with a nice salad or roasted veggies on the side. These can also be served as a side or appetizer for a taco feast (pages 104–105).

190 g/1 cup short-grain brown rice
200 g/1 cup canned chopped tomatoes in juice or puréed tomatoes
1 tablespoon finely chopped coriander/cilantro stems (leaves reserved for garnish)
olive oil, for frying and oiling the peppers

1 large red onion, sliced into half-moons
4 poblano peppers (or bell peppers if unavailable)
salt, to taste

TO SERVE
crumbled goat's cheese (optional)
Guacamole (page 104) or 1 avocado, mashed with salt and pepper

SERVES 4

Combine the rice with 415 ml/1¾ cups water and the tomatoes in a medium saucepan. Season with salt and bring to a boil. Add the coriander/cilantro stems, then reduce to a simmer and cover with a lid. Simmer for about 40 minutes until the rice is tender and the liquid has been absorbed. Remove from heat and let stand, covered, for 5 minutes.

Meanwhile, caramelize the onion by heating 1 tablespoon of oil in a large frying pan/skillet over a medium heat. Add the onion, then reduce the heat to medium-low and cook, stirring occasionally, for 20–25 minutes. Add a little water if the mixture gets dry. Stir the caramelized onion into the cooked rice and set aside.

Preheat the grill/broiler. Brush the poblanos with oil and place on a baking tray. Place under the hot grill/broiler for 3 minutes, then flip and grill again for another 3–4 minutes, until charred in places.

(Cooking times can vary, so check them often.) Allow the peppers to cool before handling.

Preheat the oven to 190°C (375°F) Gas 5. Cut the peppers open lengthwise and remove the inner white ribs and seeds. Spread out on a baking tray and spoon a portion of onion rice inside each one. Roast in the preheated oven for about 20 minutes. Serve as they are, garnished with the coriander/cilantro leaves and extra toppings of your choice.

roasted tomato date night pasta

This recipe is intended to be flexible so if you're dairy-free or vegan, omit the suggested cheese altogether. If you're eating with an omnivore, you can add the Parmesan and/or burrata to their bowl of pasta just before serving. The roasted garlicky tomatoes are also great on toast or as an extra topping for any of the bowls.

ROASTED TOMATOES

340 g/2 cups cherry or grape tomatoes, sliced in half

6–8 garlic cloves, peeled and crushed with the side of a wide knife

2 tablespoons olive oil

salt, to taste

TOMATO PASTA

175 g/6 oz. brown rice or whole-wheat pasta (I like to use spaghetti for this)

200 g/1 cup Roasted Tomatoes (from recipe above)

1–2 tablespoons olive oil

salt and freshly ground black pepper, to taste

TO SERVE

2–3 tablespoons grated Parmesan (optional)

1 ball burrata, cut in half (optional)

Walnut 'Breadcrumbs' (page 18)

a baking tray, lined with baking parchment

SERVES 2

Preheat the oven to 200°C (400°F) Gas 6. Scatter the tomatoes and garlic out on the prepared baking tray. Drizzle with the olive oil, season with salt and toss to combine. Roast in the preheated oven for 20–25 minutes, until the tomatoes have collapsed.

Towards the end of the tomato cooking time, put a large pan of water on to boil for the pasta. Once boiling, season the water with a generous amount of salt (about 1 tablespoon). Add the pasta and cook for 1 minute less than the package instructions. Drain and reserve some of the pasta cooking liquid.

Return the pasta to the pan it was cooked in and add the roasted tomatoes, a drizzle of olive oil, some salt and pepper to taste and a small splash of pasta cooking water. If you're using Parmesan, grate a couple of tablespoons in now. Toss well to combine. If it's getting a little sticky, add extra pasta water to loosen.

Portion into bowls and top each with half of the burrata (if using), black pepper and walnut 'breadcrumbs'.

sweet potato falafel

These baked falafel have a soft finish and a delicate crust rather than the crispness that comes from deep-frying. However, lots of great flavour comes from the fresh and ground herbs and spices, and they are easy to freeze and reheat when the mood strikes. I like to serve these on top of a salad, a grain bowl with a lemon tahini dressing, or in a pita with hummus, slaw and harissa.

2 medium-sized sweet potatoes (about 350 g/12 oz.)

30 g/½ tightly packed cup coriander/cilantro leaves and stems

25 g/⅓ tightly packed cup flat leaf parsley leaves

2 large spring onions/green onions, roughly chopped

3 garlic cloves, peeled

1 teaspoon ground cumin

1 teaspoon ground coriander

¼ teaspoon cayenne pepper

1 teaspoon baking powder

60 g/½ cup chickpea (gram) flour

sesame seeds, to sprinkle (optional)

salt, to taste

TO SERVE
diced cucumber
diced tomato
thinly sliced red cabbage
roughly chopped flat leaf parsley
juice of ½ lemon
freshly ground black pepper
Tahini-lemon Dressing (page 12)
pita breads

a baking tray, greased with a thin layer of olive oil

MAKES 14-16 FALAFEL TO SERVE 4 PEOPLE

Preheat the oven to 220°C (425°F) Gas 7.

Poke the sweet potatoes with a fork a couple of times and place on the oven rack in the preheated oven. Roast for 40–60 minutes, depending on the size of your sweet potatoes, until soft. Remove from the oven and allow to cool. Once cooled, peel off and discard the skin.

Meanwhile, put the coriander/cilantro, parsley, large spring onions/green onions and garlic into a small food processor and pulse until everything is finely chopped. Alternatively, you can very finely chop these ingredients with a knife.

In a large bowl, mash the sweet potato flesh with a fork, masher or hand-held mixer until smooth. Season with salt, add the spices, baking powder and chickpea (gram) flour and stir vigorously with a rubber spatula or hand-held mixer until everything is well combined. Stir in the herb, onion and garlic mixture until evenly distributed. Let the dough rest in the fridge for 20 minutes.

Preheat the oven again to 200°C (400°F) Gas 6. Scoop out portions of dough with a spoon and then lightly roll into small balls using damp hands to prevent sticking. I go for a size that is somewhere between a ping pong ball and a golf ball. Assemble the falafel on the prepared baking tray and sprinkle with sesame seeds, if using.

Bake in the preheated oven for 15–20 minutes until golden on the side touching the tray.

To serve, combine some diced cucumber, tomato, red cabbage and parsley in a bowl with the fresh lemon juice and a little salt and pepper. Serve the falafel with the cucumber-cabbage salad and tahini-lemon dressing either in a bowl or packed into a pita bread.

cauliflower steak sandwiches

My ode to an unexpectedly delicious vegetarian sandwich – the
Scuttlebutt from Saltie in Brooklyn. I love these as part of a lunch
spread, I'll serve them sliced in half with a big salad on the side.

1 medium head of
   cauliflower
120 ml/½ cup red wine
   vinegar
2 teaspoons coconut
   or cane sugar
½ teaspoon salt
1 red onion, sliced into
   thin half-moons
1 medium carrot,
   peeled into ribbons
25 g/¼ cup black
   olives, pitted and
   torn
3 tablespoons freshly
   chopped flat leaf
   parsley leaves

1 tablespoon capers,
   drained (optional)

TO SERVE
8 slices of sourdough
   bread
Creamy Chipotle Dip
   (page 17)
Cos/romaine lettuce
   leaves
crumbled feta
   (optional)

*a baking tray, greased
with a thin layer of
olive oil*

SERVES 4

Preheat the oven to 220°C (425°F) Gas 7.

Slice the head of cauliflower into thick
pieces working from the centre outwards into
2.5–4 cm/1–1½-inch pieces (these should look
like the cross section of the entire head of
cauliflower). Don't worry if these crumble a little.

Arrange the cauliflower 'steaks' on the prepared
baking tray and roast in the preheated oven for 25
minutes. Flip each piece with a spatula and return
to oven for 10 minutes until golden and tender.

Meanwhile, in a medium bowl, combine the
vinegar, sugar and salt with 120 ml/½ cup of
water. Toss the onion and carrot in the pickling
liquid and set aside for at least 20 minutes.

To serve, drain the onion and carrot and combine
in a bowl with the olives, parsley and capers
(if using). Spread the bread with creamy chipotle
dip, top with a cauliflower steak and the carrot
mixture. Finish the sandwiches with
a crisp rib of lettuce and a
little feta (if using).

POLENTA PARTY

Polenta is one of those warming and cozy dishes that, for lack of a better analogy, feels like a hug – especially when it's cold out.

A polenta party is great because you can prepare the polenta and most of the vegetables before your guests arrive. The only thing I would suggest is waiting to cook the mushrooms until just before you are ready to serve, as they're best right out of the pan and they only take a few minutes, just have your sliced mushrooms and other ingredients ready to go.

Set up a polenta bar with some of the toppings from the following recipes and include a few extra finishing touches like the ones suggested below:

This polenta party includes:

Polenta Bases (recipe right)
Roasted Courgette/Zucchini Topping (recipe right)
Seared Mushroom Topping (recipe right)
Blistered Tomato Topping (recipe right)
Herb Dressing (page 10)
good quality olive oil
cheeses such as fresh ricotta, marinated goat's cheese and shaved Pecorino
flaky sea salt and freshly ground black pepper

SERVES 6

polenta base

A note about the polenta, I use the quick-cook finely ground polenta/cornmeal, which takes about 10 minutes. I have given cooking instructions below, but check with your own package instructions as well, as cooking times may vary. I cook my polenta well in advance, to give it time to stand in the pan and thicken. It's an easy thing to do ahead and simply reheat when it's time to serve.

300 g/2 cups quick-cook (finely ground)
    dry polenta/cornmeal
235 ml/1 cup almond milk
1–2 tablespoons extra virgin olive oil
    or grass-fed butter
salt and freshly ground black pepper, to taste

Bring a large saucepan with 1.9 litres/8 cups water to the boil over a high heat. Season the water well with salt and once boiling, pour in the polenta in a steady stream, stirring constantly.

Lower the heat to medium and stir regularly for about 5 minutes until the polenta has thickened. Stir in the almond milk and cook for another 5 minutes, stirring occasionally.

Turn off the heat, stir in the olive oil or butter and some black pepper and leave, covered, to stand for at least 10 minutes.

If you cook your polenta in advance, reheat over a low heat while stirring, just before you're ready to eat.

roasted courgettes/ zucchini

2 medium courgettes/zucchini,
   cut into small, thin wedges
140 g/1 cup cooked chickpeas,
   drained, rinsed and dried
1 tablespoon olive oil
salt and freshly ground black pepper

Preheat the oven to 200°C (400°F) Gas 6.

In a large mixing bowl, combine the
courgettes/ zucchini, chickpeas and olive
oil. Season with salt and pepper and mix
to coat everything in the oil. Spread out
between one or two baking trays, as needed.
Bake in the preheated oven for 15–20 minutes
until the courgettes/zucchini are golden.

seared mushrooms

avocado oil, for frying
140 g/2 cups cremini mushrooms, cleaned
   and thinly sliced
1 tablespoon fresh thyme leaves
salt, to taste
2 teaspoons grass-fed butter (optional)

Note: I cook the ingredients in two batches to get
a better sear on the mushrooms. Cover the base
of a large frying pan/skillet with a thin layer of oil.
Tip in half the mushrooms and half the thyme.
Season with salt and cook for 3–4 minutes,
stirring once or twice, until seared. If adding
butter, add a teaspoon at the 2-minute mark,
swirling around the pan to coat the mushrooms.

Remove from the pan, transfer to a plate, and
repeat with the remaining ingredients (you will
need to add a little more oil to the pan first).

blistered tomatoes

340 g/2 cups cherry or grape tomatoes,
   sliced in half
6–8 garlic cloves, peeled and crushed with the side
   of a wide knife
2 tablespoons olive oil
salt, to taste

a baking tray, lined with baking parchment

Preheat the oven to 200°C (400°F) Gas 6. Scatter
the tomatoes and garlic out on the prepared
baking tray. Drizzle with olive oil, season with salt
and toss to combine. Roast in the preheated oven
for 20–25 minutes, until the tomatoes have
collapsed and are beginning to turn golden.

black bean & beet burgers

Against all odds, veggie burgers are having a moment. They're no longer considered an afterthought on menus or at a BBQ/cookout, they've become the main event that people line up for at trendy eateries like CHLOE and Superiority Burger in New York.

My advice: don't skimp on the toppings. I've suggested some of my favourites below, but play around with additions of your own. I find this smoky and (dare I say) meaty veggie burger works well with lots of different combinations.

olive oil, for frying
1 small red onion, finely diced
2 garlic cloves, finely chopped
2 tablespoons flax seeds
50 g/½ cup rolled oats
2 x 400-g/14-oz. cans black beans, drained and rinsed
2 medium beetroot/beets, grated
2 tablespoons tomato purée/paste
1½ teaspoons smoked paprika
1 teaspoon dried oregano
salt and freshly ground black pepper, to taste

OPTIONAL SERVING SUGGESTIONS
toasted English muffins or buns
barbecue sauce
smashed avocado
Caramelized Onions (page 18)
sliced tomato
Cos/romaine lettuce or rocket/arugula

MAKES 6-8 PATTIES

Heat a thin layer of olive oil in a medium frying pan/skillet over a medium heat. Add the onion and cook, stirring, for about 5 minutes until softened. Add the garlic and cook for 1 minute more. Remove from the heat and set aside.

In a large bowl, combine the flax seeds with 6 tablespoons water and let stand for 10 minutes.

Meanwhile, in a food processor, process the oats until they are finely chopped and bordering on a flour-like texture. Add the black beans to the food processor and pulse until they're finely chopped and combined with the oats, but not puréed.

Put the processed oats and black beans, grated beetroot/beets, cooked onions and garlic, tomato purée/paste, smoked paprika and oregano into the large bowl with the flax seeds. Season with salt and pepper and mix with a rubber spatula or with your hands until everything is well combined. Form the mixture into 6–8 patties using damp hands, making them about 2.5 cm/1 inch thick and about 7.5 cm/3–4 inches wide.

In a large frying pan/skillet, heat enough oil to cover the base over a medium-high heat. Add two patties and cook for 3–4 minutes on one side, until browned and firm. Flip and cook for another 3–4 minutes on the other side. Reduce the heat to medium if the patties are getting too charred. Remove and repeat with the remaining burgers.

Alternatively, you can lightly brush the burgers with oil and bake them on a baking tray lined with parchment paper for 25 minutes in an oven preheated to 200°C (400°F) Gas 6, flipping them halfway through the cooking time.

Serve warm on toasted English muffins or buns with plenty of your chosen toppings.

roasted aubergine/eggplant po' boys
with white bean purée & herby slaw

I believe there are two types of people in this world: those who love New Orleans, and those who don't. And by love, I don't just mean you had a good time at a bachelorette party on Bourbon Street, I mean a deep, strange pull to become a part of the city. An almost inexplicable need to learn more about it and experience it like a local.

If you haven't guessed, I'm a NOLA lover. My husband and I got married there and we love planning trips back. These po' boys are my plant-based ode to New Orleans' old school charm and its new wave of creative cuisine.

FOR THE AUBERGINE/EGGPLANT
- 1 large aubergine/ eggplant, sliced into 1.5-cm/½-inch thick rounds
- avocado or olive oil, for brushing
- 1–2 tablespoons Cajun spice mix

FOR THE WHITE BEAN PURÉE
- 160 g/1¼ cups canned white beans, drained and rinsed
- 1 tablespoon tahini
- 1 tablespoon fresh lemon juice
- ½ garlic clove, peeled
- ¼ teaspoon chilli flakes/hot red pepper flakes
- ⅛ teaspoon smoked paprika
- 1–2 tablespoons iced water (optional)
- salt, to taste

FOR THE HERBY SLAW
- 60 g/1 cup thinly sliced red cabbage
- 20 g/½ tightly packed cup flat leaf parsley or coriander/cilantro leaves (or a mixture), finely chopped
- ½ garlic clove, finely grated
- 1 tablespoon olive oil
- 2 teaspoons red wine vinegar

TO SERVE
- fresh baguettes, cut into 15-cm/6-inch lengths and split in half

a baking tray, lined with baking parchment

MAKES 2–3 BIG SANDWICHES OR 4 SMALLER ONES

Preheat the oven to 200°C (400°F) Gas 6.

Brush the aubergine/eggplant slices on both sides with oil and spread out on the prepared baking tray. Sprinkle with a little of the Cajun spice mix to give a light coating.

Roast in the preheated oven for about 15 minutes. Flip the aubergine/eggplant slices over and sprinkle the other side with Cajun spice mix. Bake for another 10 minutes, until soft and golden.

To make the white bean purée, combine all the ingredients in a food processor or blender and purée until smooth. Add the iced water for a smoother consistency.

Combine the slaw ingredients in a bowl and season to taste with salt.

Assemble the sandwiches with a good slathering of white bean purée on the baguettes, topped with the aubergine/eggplant slices and herby slaw.

baking tray pizza *with pesto winter squash*

I'm a big believer in the power of pizza. It's the ultimate laid-back, sharing food that brings people together. You will need to make the dough for this one a day in advance, but the upside is, it doesn't require any kneading.

FOR THE PIZZA DOUGH
500 g/3¾ cups 'oo' flour, plus extra for shaping
¾ teaspoon active dry yeast
2 teaspoons fine sea salt

FOR THE PESTO SQUASH TOPPING
1 winter squash (such as delicata), seeds removed and sliced into 1.5-cm/½-inch thick pieces
1 red onion, sliced into 1.5 cm/½-inch thick wedges
olive oil, for drizzling

1 whole head of garlic, base cut off to expose cloves but still attached together
100 g/½ cup Broccoli Pesto (see page 14 or store bought)
2 tablespoons olive oil
115 g/½ cup ricotta (optional)
2 large handfuls of rocket/arugula
4–6 leaves of radicchio, thinly sliced
salt, to taste

a large baking tray and a 46 x 33 cm/18 x 13 inch baking tray, both oiled

MAKES 2 PIZZAS

Make the dough a day in advance. Use a fork to mix together the flour, yeast and salt in a large mixing bowl. Slowly add 350 ml/1½ cups of water and mix together with your hands until just combined into a ball. Cover the bowl with a clean kitchen cloth and rest the dough in a warm room for at least 18 and up to 24 hours until doubled in size.

For the pizza topping, preheat the oven to 200°C (400°F) Gas 6. Arrange the squash and onion on the first prepared baking tray and season with salt. Drizzle a square of foil with a little oil and use this to wrap the head of garlic into a parcel. Put the parcel on the tray with the squash and roast in the preheated oven for 25 minutes until tender. When cool, remove the soft garlic pulp from its skin and set aside.

Punch the pizza dough down a little to deflate it. Dust a clean work surface with flour, tip out the dough and cut in half. Slowly stretch one of the balls of dough into a rectangle with your hands and put on the second prepared baking tray. Continue to stretch the dough until it almost fits the size of the baking tray. Patch any major holes in the dough, but don't worry about making it perfect, it should be fairly thin though.

Preheat the oven to its highest setting and position the oven rack in the middle.

Mix the pesto with the 2 tablespoons oil and spread half across the dough. Put the pizza in the oven, then lower the heat to 230°C (450°F) Gas 8. Bake for 12–15 minutes until starting to turn golden at the edges. Remove from the oven.

Preheat the grill/broiler. Top the pizza with half the roasted garlic cloves, lightly squashing them with a fork. If using ricotta, dollop teaspoons of half across the dough. Scatter half the roasted squash and onions on the pizza.

Grill/broil for 2 minutes and remove when browned in places – watch carefully to make sure it doesn't burn. Your dough should be cooked through and mostly golden. Top with half the rocket/arugula and radicchio. Cool for 5 minutes, then cut into squares. Repeat with the other half of the dough and remaining ingredients.

vegetable paella

My dad is actually the paella master in our family. He's made it for all the big family parties for years, and gets it right every time. It helps that he's also a fisherman and always gets the best shellfish to include.

My humble veggie version is easier to make but has a similar flavour base from the golden saffron, tomatoes, piquillo peppers and smoked paprika.

FOR THE MUSHROOM VEGETABLE BROTH
950 ml/4 cups vegetable stock/broth
10 g/⅓ cup mixed dried mushrooms
5 garlic cloves, skins left on and crushed with the side of a wide knife

FOR THE BASE
1 medium onion, roughly chopped
3 garlic cloves, peeled
1 medium tomato, quartered
2 roasted piquillo red peppers from a jar, drained
2 tablespoons olive oil
1 teaspoon sherry vinegar
1 teaspoon smoked paprika (I used sweet but spicy is good too)
salt, to taste

FOR THE VEGETABLES
olive oil, for frying
225 g/8 oz. mixed mushrooms (cremini, portobello, oyster are all good here), sliced
1 fennel bulb, thinly sliced lengthwise
1 small or ½ large red (bell) pepper, deseeded and cut into strips
1 small or ½ large yellow (bell) pepper, deseeded and cut into strips
100 g/¾ cup frozen peas, thawed

FOR THE RICE
2 tablespoons olive oil
240 g/1¼ heaped cups Arborio rice
generous pinch of saffron threads

SERVES 4

For the broth, pour the vegetable stock/broth into a saucepan with the dried mushrooms and garlic. Cover and bring to a boil. Simmer, covered, for 15–20 minutes, then remove from the heat and let stand until needed. When ready to use the stock/broth, remove and discard the mushrooms and garlic with a slotted spoon and gently reheat.

Meanwhile, pulse the base ingredients in a food processor until finely chopped but not puréed.

For the vegetables, heat about 2 tablespoons oil in a paella pan or large frying pan/skillet with high sides. Add the mushrooms and season with salt. Cook over a medium heat for about 3–5 minutes, until tender and golden. Set aside.

Add a little more oil, the fennel and (bell) peppers and season with salt. Cook, stirring a few times, until caramelized and tender (about 5–7 minutes). Remove from the pan and set aside on a plate.

For the rice, heat the olive oil over a medium heat in the same pan. Add the rice and cook for 1–2 minutes, stirring, until the rice is coated in oil and almost translucent. Stir in the tomato-onion base and cook for 2 minutes. Add the mushroom and vegetable stock/broth and the saffron. Make sure the rice is in an even layer across the pan.

Turn the heat up to medium-high and cook for 20–25 minutes, uncovered, without stirring, until the rice is al dente. You should hear a slight popping sound towards the end, which means a delicious crispy crust is forming at the bottom.

Place the cooked vegetables (including peas) on top of the cooked rice, turn off the heat and cover the pan with a clean kitchen cloth. Let stand for 5 minutes. Serve warm straight from the pan.

roasted vegetable ratatouille

Ratatouille really is a celebration of vegetables. I've tried so many variations on the recipe and enjoyed all of them in their own way. But this two-baking tray, hands-off version is the one I make the most.

It's easy to throw together and goes from good to great when you let everything cool in a big bowl together. It's especially good one, two and three days later.

It's a handy recipe for stress-free entertaining. I like making it the day before having people over for a polenta or a bruschetta (or anything starchy) party.

1 Italian aubergine/ eggplant
1 medium red (bell) pepper
2 courgettes/zucchini
340 g/2 cups cherry tomatoes
1 red onion
6–7 garlic cloves
1 tablespoon fresh rosemary leaves, finely chopped
2 teaspoons fresh thyme leaves
salt, to taste

2 baking trays, oiled

SERVES 4

Preheat the oven to 200°C (400°F) Gas 6.

Cut the aubergine/eggplant, red (bell) pepper and courgettes/zucchini into 1.5-cm/½-inch pieces.

Slice the cherry tomatoes in half. Slice the red onion into 1.5-cm/½-inch wide wedges. Smash the garlic cloves with the flat part of a wide knife to break but not remove the skins.

Spread the vegetables out on the two prepared baking trays, leaving some space in between each vegetable (you may have to do this in batches). Sprinkle evenly with the rosemary and thyme and season with salt.

Roast in the preheated oven for 15 minutes, then rotate the trays, flip the vegetables, and roast for another 15 minutes. You want the vegetables to be golden and just starting to caramelize in places.

Once you take the baking trays out of the oven, leave to stand for 5 minutes, then transfer the vegetables to a large bowl. Mix everything together and allow to cool to room temperature. cover and place in the fridge to store and bring up to room temperature before serving.

mushroom & lentil no-meat-balls

This recipe is inspired by The Meatball Shop in New York, which is (maybe surprisingly) very vegetable-lover friendly. These no-meatballs aren't pretending to be something they're not, rather they taste like the umami-rich mushrooms, herbs, spices and earthy lentils that they're made from.

They're great for everything from salads, to pasta, to appetizers, and play well with both tomato sauces and pestos – giving you plenty of options. One of my favourite ways to serve is as a meatball slider.

170 g/1 cup dried green lentils
700–900 ml/3–4 cups water or vegetable stock/broth
olive oil, for frying
1 red onion, finely diced
3 garlic cloves, finely chopped
1 teaspoon dried oregano
¼ teaspoon fennel seeds
2 tablespoons ground chia seeds
140 g/2 cups of mushrooms (baby portabello or cremini work great for this), roughly chopped

50 g/⅓ cup raw walnuts, roughly chopped
1 tablespoon tomato purée/paste
2 tablespoons oat flour
salt, to taste

TO SERVE (OPTIONAL)
seeded rolls
Broccoli Pesto (page 14)
tomato sauce
rocket/arugula

a baking tray, lined with baking parchment

MAKES 12-14

In a large saucepan, combine the lentils with the water or vegetable stock/broth (enough to generously cover the lentils). Add a pinch of salt and bring to a boil. Reduce the heat and simmer over a medium-low heat for 20–25 minutes until tender but not mushy. Once cooked, drain.

In a large frying pan/skillet, heat enough olive oil to cover the base of the pan over a medium-high heat. Cook the onion for 4–5 minutes, stirring occasionally, until softened and translucent. Add the garlic, oregano and fennel seeds and season with salt. Cook for another minute until fragrant.

Meanwhile, combine the ground chia seeds with 6 tablespoons of water in a small bowl and leave to stand for at least 5 minutes.

In a food processor or blender, combine the cooked lentils, mushrooms, cooked onion mixture, walnuts, tomato purée/paste, chia seeds and oat flour. Process to a rough, slightly chunky dough, scraping down the sides a couple of times.

Preheat the oven to 180°C (350°F) Gas 4.

Form the mixture into golf ball-sized balls and arrange close together on the prepared baking tray. Bake in the preheated oven for 30 minutes until slightly browned and warmed through. Great served as sliders in rolls with pesto, tomato sauce and rocket/arugula, if desired.

farro risotto with green peas

Farro risotto, or farrotto, uses this sturdy grain in the place of short-grain rice and adds a pleasant nuttiness and texture to a risotto. Puréed peas add sweetness, protein and a vibrant green that looks irresistible.

1 teaspoon chopped
   dried porcini or
   shiitake mushrooms
950 ml/4 cups
   vegetable stock/
   broth
2 tablespoons olive oil
   or butter
2 medium leeks, white
   and light green parts
   only, thinly sliced
   into half-moons
4 garlic cloves, finely
   chopped
185 g/1 cup farro

FOR THE PEA PURÉE
125 g/1 cup frozen peas
2 big handfuls of fresh
   spinach
1 tablespoon fresh
   lemon juice
salt, to taste

FOR THE GARNISHES
grated Parmesan
   (optional)
toasted pine nuts
fresh basil, finely
   chopped

SERVES 4

In a medium saucepan, combine the dried mushrooms and vegetable stock/broth and bring to a gentle simmer.

Meanwhile, in a large saucepan with high sides or in a Dutch oven, heat the olive oil or butter over a medium-high heat. Add the leeks and garlic and cook, stirring, for about 6–8 minutes until the leeks are softened, adding a little splash of water if the mixture becomes too dry.

Add the farro and stir to coat in the olive oil and leeks and toast for about 2 minutes. Add the stock/broth one ladle-ful at a time, every 3–4 minutes, stirring once or twice and then letting it bubble until the liquid evaporates. Repeat until all the stock/broth has been added and the farro is tender and creamy, about 40 minutes.

Meanwhile, thaw the frozen peas in a medium bowl by pouring boiling water over to submerge and covering with a lid. Leave to stand for 5 minutes. Drain and transfer the peas to a blender or food processor. Add the spinach, a pinch or two of salt and the lemon juice. Purée until smooth-ish (I would encourage some chunks). You can add a tablespoon of warm water or stock/broth if needed to move things along.

Finish the farro risotto by stirring in some Parmesan (if using) and dividing among bowls. Top each bowl with the pea purée and swirl it in to incorporate. Top with toasted pine nuts, basil and more Parmesan, if desired.

sweet potato dumplings

This hearty dumpling soup is a great meal on its own, but you can also serve it with some stir-fried veggies and sushi rice on the side.

1 large sweet potato
1 tablespoon olive oil
½ red onion or whole shallot, finely diced
3 garlic cloves, finely chopped
¼–½ teaspoon chilli flakes/hot red pepper flakes
1 tablespoon tamari
20–25 ready-made wonton/dumpling wrappers
8 heads of baby pak choi/bok choy or stalks baby broccoli, sliced in half OR
4 medium heads of pak choi/bok choy, quartered

475 ml/2 cups boiling water or vegetable stock/broth
950 ml/4 cups boiling water or vegetable stock/broth
4 tablespoons white miso paste

TO SERVE
3 large spring onions/green onions, thinly sliced
chilli flakes/hot red pepper flakes
soft-boiled eggs (optional)

SERVES 4-5 (MAKES 20-25 DUMPLINGS)

Preheat the oven to 220°C (425°F) Gas 7.

Poke the sweet potato with a fork, then place on the oven rack and cook in the preheated oven for 40–60 minutes until soft. Remove from the oven and allow to cool. (You can do this a day in advance if you like.) Peel and discard the skin and mash the flesh in a medium mixing bowl with a fork.

In a small frying pan/skillet, heat the olive oil over a medium heat. Add the onion and garlic and cook, stirring, for about 4–6 minutes until softened. Stir in the chilli flakes/hot red pepper flakes and remove from the heat. Add the cooked onion mixture and tamari to the mashed sweet potato and stir well. This will be the filling for your dumplings.

Place about a heaped teaspoon of sweet potato filling in the middle of each dumpling wrapper, adding a little more if needed. Have a little bowl of water handy and use a finger to dampen along half of the dumpling wrapper's edge. Fold in half and crimp along the edge by pinching the dough together to seal the dumpling wrapper closed.

Line the bottom of a large saucepan or Dutch oven with some of the pak choi/bok choy or baby broccoli. Pour over 350 ml/1½ cups of boiling water or vegetable stock/broth. Place the dumplings into the pan on top of the vegetables, cover with a lid and cook over a medium heat for 2–3 minutes until the wrappers are transparent. Note: You will have to do this in batches.

You may run out of vegetables before dumplings and that's okay – just make sure that the dumplings aren't completely submerged in the water when you steam them on their own. They should have about 1.5 cm/½ inch of water, so you may need to remove some of the water from the pan after you've cooked all of the vegetables.

Remove the dumplings and vegetables with a slotted spoon and divide among bowls. Repeat with remaining veggies and dumplings. Once all dumplings are cooked, add 950 ml/4 more cups of boiling water or stock/broth to the pan and bring to a boil. Whisk in the miso paste and ladle the stock/broth over the bowls with the dumplings.

Serve the bowls scattered with the chopped spring onions/green onions, chilli flakes/hot red pepper flakes and soft-boiled eggs (if using).

SAVOURY SNACKS
FOR SHARING

Dishes that involve dipping, crunching and
extra toppings make the best kind of snacks.
Serve these to kick off a dinner or serve cocktail
party-style with drinks.

oven-baked rosemary crisps/chips

DIY oven crisps/chips are way prettier than the ones that come in a package. I highly recommend using a mandoline for slicing your beetroots/beets and potatoes because if they're not thin enough, they won't crisp up.

I mention salt to taste (instead of an exact amount) because I find it easier to use a salt shaker here to distribute the salt in smaller quantities.

Try serving these tasty crisps/chips with any of the Hummus recipes on pages 144–145 for dipping.

2 small-medium beetroot/beets
1 sweet potato, white potato or purple potato
olive oil, for brushing
1 tablespoon fresh rosemary leaves, finely chopped
salt, to taste
any of the Hummus recipes (pages 144–145), to serve

2 baking sheets, brushed with oil

SERVES 3-4

Preheat the oven to 190°C (375°F) Gas 5.

Slice the beetroot/beets and potato very thinly (preferably with a mandoline).

Arrange the individual beetroot/beet and potato slices on the prepared baking sheets, giving each slice plenty of space.

Lightly brush the vegetables with a little olive oil. Sprinkle with the rosemary and season with salt to taste.

Bake in the preheated oven for 10–13 minutes, watching them carefully to make sure they don't burn. Remove from the oven and let the crisps/chips cool on the sheets before transferring to a serving plate or bowl. Repeat with any remaining vegetables as necessary. Serve with a big bowl of hummus for dipping, if you like.

sweet potato wedges
with garlic yogurt sauce

If there's one thing that almost every Aussie pub does well (besides ice cold beer), it's potato wedges. A step up from fries or crisps/chips, wedges have a bit more heft to them, often have more seasoning, and actually resemble a potato with a bit of skin still visible.

Wedges are usually served with a blend of sour cream and sweet chilli sauce and are best eaten while looking out at the ocean.

This is my at-home version. Sweet potatoes are cut into wedges and sprinkled with a good spice blend (I used Old Bay to give it an American seaside twist, but you can use a Cajun spice mix or your favourite paprika-based blend) and a little bit of dry polenta/cornmeal for texture.

Greek yogurt made savoury with a little salt, garlic and olive oil is the perfect dip. It's similar to sour cream, but you get a good probiotic and protein bump from the yogurt. I like to swirl in a little sriracha or sweet chilli sauce to replicate the real thing.

I also like to serve these with Creamy Chipotle Dip (Page 17) or Basic Avocado Dip (Page 17).

2 sweet potatoes, scrubbed clean and cut lengthwise into 2.5-cm/1-inch wedges
1 tablespoon olive oil
1 tablespoon Old Bay or similar spice blend such as Cajun
1 tablespoon polenta/cornmeal (optional)
salt, to taste

TO SERVE (OPTIONAL)
Garlic Yogurt Dip (page 17)
your favourite hot sauce or sweet chilli sauce

SERVES 4

Preheat the oven to 220°C (425°F) Gas 7.

In a large bowl, toss the sweet potato wedges with the oil to evenly coat. Sprinkle with your chosen spice blend and the polenta/cornmeal. Season with salt to taste and toss again to coat the potatoes well.

Lay out the wedges on two baking trays, leaving at least 2.5 cm/1 inch in between each piece. If you only have one tray, do it in two batches.

Bake in the preheated oven for 15 minutes. Remove from the oven and flip the sweet potatoes over. Bake for another 10–15 minutes. The wedges should be golden, a little crispy on the outside and soft on the inside.

Serve the sweet potato wedges warm with garlic yogurt dip and hot sauce or sweet chilli sauce, if desired.

basic hummus

Start with this base, then add other ingredients to make your own signature flavour combinations.

210 g/1½ cups cooked chickpeas or
1 x 400-g/14-oz. can chickpeas, drained and rinsed
2 heaped tablespoons tahini

juice of half a small lemon
1 small garlic clove, peeled
3–4 tablespoons ice cold water
salt, to taste

SERVES 4-6

Put the chickpeas, tahini, lemon juice and garlic in a food processor. Add salt to taste. Purée for 1–3 minutes, scraping down the sides once or twice with a rubber spatula as you go.

Add 2–3 tablespoons of ice cold water to the mixture to help give it a smooth but fluffy texture. Add more ice cold water as needed until you reach the desired consistency.

spicy green hummus

olive oil for frying, plus extra to serve
1 small garlic clove, chopped
1 jalapeño, seeds and inner ribs discarded, chopped
70 g/½ cup canned chickpeas, drained and rinsed
60 g/½ cup shelled edamame beans

2 heaped tablespoons tahini
juice of half a lime
15 g/½ packed cup coriander/cilantro, plus extra to serve
3–4 tablespoons ice cold water
salt, to taste

SERVES 4-6

In a frying pan/skillet, heat 1 tablespoon olive oil over a medium heat. Add the garlic and jalapeño and cook for about 5 minutes until softened. Remove from the heat and stand for 5 minutes.

Place everything except the ice cold water (including the jalapeño, garlic and cooking oil) in a food processor and blend, scraping down the sides once or twice. Add the ice cold water slowly until you reach the desired smooth but fluffy consistency. Serve with a drizzle of olive oil and chopped coriander/cilantro on top, if desired.

butternut & harissa hummus

1 tablespoon olive oil
2 garlic cloves, finely chopped
½ teaspoon ground cumin
140 g/½ cup roasted, mashed butternut squash
140 g/1 cup canned chickpeas, drained and rinsed

2 heaped tablespoons tahini
juice of half a lemon
3–4 tablespoons ice cold water
salt, to taste
1 teaspoon harissa paste mixed with 1 tablespoon olive oil

SERVES 4-6

In a small frying pan/skillet, heat the olive oil, garlic and cumin over a medium heat until the garlic is sizzling and fragrant. Remove from the heat and let stand for 5 minutes.

In a food processor, combine the squash, chickpeas, tahini, lemon juice and the cooked garlic and cumin with the oil from the pan. Season with salt. Blend for 1–3 minutes, scraping down the sides with a rubber spatula. Add the ice cold water slowly until you reach the desired smooth but fluffy consistency. Place the hummus in a bowl and pour over the harissa oil to serve.

za'atar & pine nut hummus

210 g/1½ cups canned
   chickpeas or 1 x 400-g/
   14-oz. can chickpeas,
   drained and rinsed
2 heaped tablespoons tahini
juice of half a lemon
1 small garlic clove, peeled
3–4 tablespoons ice cold
   water
salt, to taste

25 g/¼ cup Kalamata olives,
   pitted and finely chopped
2 tablespoon pine nuts,
   toasted
1 tablespoon extra virgin
   olive oil
1 teaspoon Za'atar
   (page 81)

SERVES 4-6

Put the chickpeas, tahini, lemon juice and garlic in a
food processor. Season with salt. Blend for 1–3 minutes,
scraping down the sides once or twice with a rubber
spatula. Add the ice cold water slowly until you reach
the desired smooth but fluffy consistency.

Top with the olives, toasted pine nuts, olive oil and
za'atar to serve.

piadinas

Piadinas are basically an Italian version of a quesadilla – toasted tortillas folded and filled with modest amounts of flavourful ingredients.

I was first introduced to them when Fabian and I were living in Bondi Beach in Sydney. There's a tiny little spot (called La Piadina) a couple of streets away from the ocean that serves up freshly made piadina with top quality Italian goodies.

I have yet to find piadina as good in New York, so for now I'll settle for my own plant-centric version.

**FOR THE BUTTERNUT
& FENNEL FILLING**
1 fennel bulb, sliced lengthwise into thin 1.5-cm/½-inch pieces
250 g/2 cups diced butternut squash
salt, to taste
Caramelized Onions (page 18)

**FOR THE WHITE BEAN
& BALSAMIC FILLING**
120 ml/½ cup balsamic vinegar
250 g/1½ cups canned white beans, drained and rinsed

1 teaspoon freshly chopped rosemary
2 teaspoons olive oil
Roasted Tomatoes with Garlic (page 112)
1–2 handfuls of baby rocket/arugula

FOR THE PIADINAS
8 spelt or whole-wheat wraps or tortillas

a baking tray, oiled

MAKES ABOUT 8 PIADINA

Preheat the oven to 200°C (400°F) Gas 6.

Arrange the fennel slices on the prepared baking tray and roast in the preheated oven for 20–25 minutes, flipping the slices halfway through.

Meanwhile, steam or boil the butternut squash cubes for about 8–10 minutes until tender. Drain, if needed, and season with salt. Set aside.

Put the balsamic vinegar in a small saucepan over a medium heat. Simmer for about 5 minutes until reduced by half and syrupy. Set aside until needed.

Place the white beans and rosemary in a medium saucepan with 60 ml/¼ cup of water. Season with salt and cook over a medium heat, stirring, for about 5 minutes. While you're stirring, lightly mash the white beans with a fork, adding a little more water if the mixture gets too dry. Remove from the heat when the water has thickened and continue to mash with a fork until most of the beans are broken apart. Stir in the olive oil and add extra salt to taste, if needed.

When you have finished preparing one or both of your fillings, heat a cast iron pan or griddle/grill pan over a medium heat. Place a wrap on the dry pan for about 2 minutes until starting to brown. Flip the wrap over.

Add your chosen filling on one half of the wrap, but don't overstuff. The butternut squash should be slightly mashed down on the wrap with a fork to make sure it stays put. Top the butternut with the roasted fennel and some caramelized onions.

For the white bean and balsamic filling, spread a couple of heaped spoonfuls of beans onto one half of the wrap, top with roasted tomatoes, rocket/arugula and a little syrupy balsamic.

Fold the other half of the wrap over to create a semi-circle with the filling inside. Flip to make sure the wrap is golden brown and slightly crispy on both sides. Slice in half and serve warm. Repeat with the remaining wraps and fillings.

vegetable-loaded nachos

For such a communal food, what defines good nachos is often a very personal thing. The exact quantities for your nacho toppings will vary depending on the size of your nacho tray and your preference.

The Barbecue Black Beans and Creamy Chipotle Dip make more than you'll need for these nachos, but luckily they're great in tacos, burritos and salads, too.

I like to serve these nachos directly on the tray, but you could also serve them by transferring the baking parchment onto a large plate.

250 g/2 cups butternut squash, cut into small 1.5 cm/½-inch cubes
1 tablespoon olive or avocado oil
½ teaspoon dried and ground chipotle or cayenne pepper
tortilla chips
200 g/1 cup Barbecue Black Beans (page 9), plus more as needed
salt, to taste

TO SERVE
115 g/½ cup guacamole (or avocado mashed with salt and pepper), plus more on the side
130 g/½ cup pico de gallo (or fresh salsa)
50 g/¼ cup Creamy Chipotle Dip (Page 17)
3 spring onions/scallions, thinly sliced

a baking tray, lined with baking parchment

SERVES 4-6

Preheat the oven to 200°C (400°F) Gas 6.

In a large bowl, toss the butternut squash cubes with the oil, ground chipotle or cayenne pepper and a sprinkling of salt to taste. Spread out evenly on a baking tray and roast in the preheated oven for about 25 minutes until golden and tender.

Turn the oven temperature down to 180°C (350°F) Gas 4.

Spread the tortilla chips out on the lined baking tray – enough to fill the tray generously in a thin layer. Scatter over the roasted butternut and then the barbecue black beans, spreading them out evenly across the tray. Bake in the preheated oven for about 10 minutes.

Remove the tray from the oven and top the nachos with small dollops of guacamole or mashed avocado and pico de gallo or salsa, a drizzle of chipotle tahini sauce and a scattering of spring onions/scallions. Serve immediately either directly from the tray or transfer to a large plate.

BRUSCHETTA PARTY

A bruschetta party is basically just a snack board on steroids. The number one necessity for a bruschetta night is good bread. Fresh baguettes work well, because slices are smaller, allowing people to try a bunch of different toppings. I really love the buckwheat and sourdough baguettes from my local bakery for added depth of flavour.

Besides the white bean & kale dip (which I like to serve warm), everything else can and should be served at room temperature, making a bruschetta party perhaps the most laid-back of all dinner parties.

I like putting out a few crudites (such as sliced radishes and carrots) to offer a non-bread option for dipping. Along with these plant-based toppings, some creamy additions like fresh ricotta, burrata or mozzarella are usually welcome and - magically - dinner is served.

This bruschetta party includes:

fresh baguettes, sliced and lightly toasted
Tomato Basil Salsa (recipe right)
White Bean & Kale Dip (recipe right)
Melted Courgette/Zucchini & Leek Dip
   (recipe right)
Guacamole (page 104)
vegetable crudités
cheeses such as fresh ricotta, burrata
   and mozzarella

SERVES 6

tomato basil salsa

Summer is the time for this classic bruschetta topping. Only make this one when you can get really great fresh tomatoes, otherwise skip it.

450 g/1 lb. tomatoes (whichever kind you have
   to hand), halved and most of the seeds cut out,
   then finely diced
20 g/½ lightly packed cup basil leaves, finely
   chopped
1 garlic clove, grated
2 tablespoons good olive oil
1 teaspoon sherry vinegar
salt, to taste

Combine all the ingredients together in a medium mixing bowl. Leave to stand for 15 minutes to let the flavours mingle. Taste and adjust the seasoning as desired.

white bean & kale dip

This substantial and warming dip is great for the colder months.

1 fennel bulb, trimmed and sliced lengthwise into 1.5-cm/½-inch thick pieces

6 garlic cloves, lightly crushed with the side of a wide knife, skins left on

60 g/1 cup kale, stems removed and roughly chopped

1 x 400-g/14-oz. can white beans, drained and rinsed

1 tablespoon olive oil, plus more to serve

salt and freshly ground black pepper, to taste

25 g/⅓ cup Parmesan (optional)

a baking tray, oiled

Preheat the oven to 200°C (400°F) Gas 6.

Arrange the fennel and garlic on the prepared baking tray and sprinkle with salt. Roast in the preheated oven for 20–25 minutes, turning over halfway, until the fennel is golden and tender. Remove from the oven and cool slightly. Remove the garlic pulp and discard the skin.

Meanwhile, steam the kale (in a steamer basket or a large pan with a small amount of boiling water) for about 1 minute until slightly wilted.

In a food processor, combine the white beans with the steamed kale, roasted fennel and garlic pulp, olive oil and some salt and pepper. Blend to a smooth purée. Adjust the seasoning to taste.

Transfer to an ovenproof dish. If adding Parmesan, preheat the grill/broiler. Sprinkle Parmesan on top and grill for 2–3 minutes until golden. If not adding cheese, bake for 10 minutes in an oven preheated to 180°C (350°F) Gas 4 and serve warm, drizzled with olive oil if desired.

melted courgette/ zucchini & leek dip

This recipe is great for the bruschetta party, but can also be stirred into warm pasta or a sturdy grain like farro or brown rice.

I use a mandoline to quickly slice the courgette/zucchini very thin. A good chef's knife and an extra couple of minutes will do just fine in its place, though!

olive oil, for frying

1 large leek, thinly sliced

3 courgettes/zucchini or summer squash (or a mix), thinly sliced

3 garlic cloves, finely chopped

1 tablespoon fresh lemon juice

pinch of chilli flakes/ hot red pepper flakes

salt and freshly ground black pepper, to taste

freshly chopped mint leaves, to serve

In a large pan with high sides, heat a generous glug of olive oil over a medium heat. Add the leek and season with salt. Cook for 5–7 minutes, stirring occasionally, until the leek begins to soften. Add a splash of water if the pan gets dry.

Add the courgettes/zucchini and garlic to the pan and stir. Reduce the heat to medium-low. Cook, uncovered, for about 10–15 minutes, stirring every so often and adding a bit of water if anything sticks. It's ready when the courgettes/zucchini are almost falling apart and there is no excess water.

Stir in the lemon juice and chilli flakes/hot red pepper flakes and remove from the heat. Season with black pepper and scatter over fresh mint leaves to serve.

DESSERTS & SWEET TREATS

Ending on a sweet note is how I prefer to roll.
I think if you want dessert every day, you should
have it. These treats focus on fruits, alternative
flours, nuts and seeds for a plant-centric twist.

chickpea & chocolate chip cookies

These chewy and chocolatey cookies are the dessert I always want on-hand. They get their great (dairy-free and egg-free) texture from coconut oil, have just the right amount of sweetness, and use protein-rich chickpea (gram) flour, which leaves me feeling truly satisfied.

2 tablespoons ground chia seeds
120 ml/½ cup gently melted coconut oil
100 g/½ cup coconut sugar or soft light brown sugar
1 teaspoon vanilla extract
185 g/1½ cups chickpea (gram) flour
1 teaspoon baking powder
¼ teaspoon salt
50 g/⅓ cup 70% dark/bittersweet chocolate chips or roughly chopped chocolate
flaky sea salt, for sprinkling on top (optional)

a baking tray, lined with baking parchment

MAKES ABOUT 12

In a large bowl, combine the ground chia seeds with 6 tablespoons of water and whisk to combine; this should form a gel-like consistency.

Add the melted coconut oil to the bowl with the chia seeds, along with the sugar and vanilla. Whisk with a hand-held electric whisk until well combined.

In a separate medium bowl, combine the chickpea (gram) flour, baking powder and salt. Add these dry ingredients to the wet ingredients and mix to combine everything using a rubber spatula. (Your cookie batter will be slightly wetter than a typical cookie batter, but don't worry.) Stir in the chocolate chips or chopped chocolate until evenly dispersed. Place the batter in the fridge to firm up for 30–60 minutes.

Preheat the oven to 180°C (350°F) Gas 4.

Scoop the chilled mixture into ping pong-sized balls, using a spoon, and space evenly apart on the prepared baking tray. Press each cookie gently using a piece of baking parchment and your hand to flatten them slightly. Sprinkle each cookie with a small pinch of sea salt (if using).

Bake in the preheated oven for 11–12 minutes (if they look a little underdone, that's okay). Remove from the oven and leave to cool on the baking tray for 5–10 minutes before transferring to a wire rack to cool fully. Store in an airtight container at room temperature for up to 5 days.

strawberry crumble cups

Crumbles are an easy way to cook with seasonal fruit - this recipe also works well with peaches, blueberries, apples or pears, depending on the time of year.

It's also a great way to use sub-par fruit that might not quite be in season yet. The time in the oven will make it sweeter and softer and the nutty crumble topping adds a crunchy contrast in texture.

Roasted strawberries in particular, taste like straight-up candy - no extra sugar needed - making them the perfect base for a low-maintenance crumble. Serve these with a little coconut cream or vanilla ice cream.

I like to make a double batch of the crumble topping and store it in the freezer to top seasonal fruit with on a whim for a fast dessert fix.

200 g/2 cups strawberries, sliced into 1.5-cm/½-inch thick pieces
100 g/1 cup almond flour
50 g/½ cup rolled oats
½ teaspoon ground cinnamon
pinch of salt
60 ml/¼ cup gently melted coconut oil, plus extra for greasing
1 tablespoon maple syrup
whipped coconut cream or ice cream, to serve

4 small ramekins, greased with coconut oil
baking tray, lined with foil or baking parchment

SERVES 4

Preheat the oven to 180°C (350°F) Gas 4.

Divide the strawberries between the ramekins, fitting them in snugly (they will reduce a little as they cook)

In a medium mixing bowl, combine the almond flour, oats, cinnamon and salt. Add the melted coconut oil and maple syrup and mix until everything is well coated. Divide the crumble mixture between the four greased ramekins, packing it tightly.

Put the ramekins on the prepared baking tray and bake in the preheated oven for 30–35 minutes, until the strawberries are bubbling at the edges and the crumble toppings are golden and crispy.

Remove from the oven and leave to cool for 15–20 minutes before serving with whipped coconut cream or ice cream.

poached apples *with maple pecans*

Simple juice-poached cinnamon apples make the most of natural sweetness. Serve these warm with the creamy topping of your choice and don't skip the maple pecans – they're super easy and make for good snacking if you have some leftover.

2 sweet apples (I would use Honeycrisp or Pink Lady for this)
½ teaspoon ground cinnamon
235–350 ml/1–1½ cups unfiltered apple juice
40 g/⅓ cup pecans, roughly chopped
1 teaspoon coconut oil
1 teaspoon maple syrup
vanilla ice cream, whipped cream or yogurt, to serve (optional)

SERVES 4

Preheat the oven to 180°C (350°F) Gas 4.

Cut the apples in half widthways and scoop out the seeds in the centre with a spoon to create a little well. Sprinkle the white apple flesh with cinnamon.

In a small roasting pan with high sides (I use a 20 x 20-cm/8 x 8-inch one), place the apples face-down and pour in the apple juice, making sure that it covers the entire base of the roasting pan and comes a quarter to a third of the way up the apples. Bake in the preheated oven for 45–55 minutes until the apples are tender.

Meanwhile, toast the pecans in a dry frying pan/skillet over a medium-low heat for about 4–5 minutes, tossing a few times, until fragrant and beginning to turn golden.

Move the pecans to one side of the pan to clear a little space. Add the coconut oil and allow to melt. Add the maple syrup and stir into the oil using a rubber spatula (it should be bubbling a bit). Stir to combine and evenly coat the pecans. Remove from the heat and transfer the pecans onto a piece of baking parchment. Leave to cool and set fully before serving (I pop them in the fridge to speed the cooling time if the kitchen is warm).

Serve the poached apples topped with the pecans and ice cream (vegan ice cream is encouraged), whipped cream or yogurt.

coconut cream peach parfaits

Coconut cream and granola can be the base for any fruit dessert. If peaches or nectarines aren't in season, try your favourite berries or sliced banana for banana cream pie-esque parfaits.

FOR THE MAPLE CRUNCH GRANOLA

140 g/1½ cups rolled oats

115 g/1 cup mixed nuts and seeds (such as pecans and pumpkin seeds)

25 g/¼ cup ground almonds/almond meal

1 tablespoon chia seeds

1 teaspoon ground cinnamon

¼ teaspoon ground cardamom

¼ teaspoon salt

60 ml/¼ cup melted coconut oil

60 ml/¼ cup maple syrup

1 teaspoon vanilla extract

FOR THE PARFAIT

100–120 g/¾–1 cup Maple Crunch Granola (above)

1 x 400-g/14-oz. can full fat coconut milk, cooled in the fridge overnight

2 teaspoons maple syrup

½ teaspoon vanilla extract

2 ripe peaches, cut in half, pitted and thinly sliced

large baking tray, lined with baking parchment
4 x small jars or glasses (a 235 ml/1-cup capacity works well)

MAKES 4

Preheat the oven to 170°C (325°F) Gas 3.

For the granola, in a large bowl mix together the oats, nuts and seeds, ground almonds/almond meal, chia seeds, cinnamon, cardamom and salt.

In a pourable measuring cup or jug, combine the melted coconut oil with the maple syrup and vanilla.

Pour the wet ingredients into the dry and mix until well combined. Spread out evenly on the prepared baking tray and bake in the preheated oven for 35–40 minutes, rotating the tray halfway. Leave to cool fully on the tray before breaking up by hand. Store in a jar until needed.

For the parfait, put a large mixing bowl in the freezer for a few minutes.

Put a layer of crumbled granola into the base of the four small jars or glasses.

Scoop out the hardened coconut cream from the top of the can (reserving the coconut water for something else) and put the cream in the chilled mixing bowl. Whip for 1–2 minutes using an electric whisk until light and smooth. Add the maple syrup and vanilla and whisk again to combine for about 1 minute more.

Put a layer of cream into each of the small containers, followed by a layer of peach slices. Top this with more granola and repeat until filled. Refrigerate until ready to serve. Sprinkle with extra granola just before serving.

chocolate banana bread

Until I met my husband, banana-flavoured anything just wasn't my thing. Somehow his love of a banana-chocolate pairing rubbed off on me, and I find myself in the mood for this banana bread all the time.

You can definitely eat this for breakfast - it's free of refined sugar and dairy and high in fibre - and a little scattering of chocolate never ruined anyone's morning! It's great with some peanut or almond butter spread on a slice, too.

I've placed this recipe in the desserts chapter, though, because I like to serve it like cake - warm and à la mode.

130 g/1 cup whole-wheat flour
100 g/1 cup almond flour
50 g/½ cup oat flour (or 70 g/generous ½ cup oats, finely ground)
3 teaspoons baking powder
1 teaspoon ground cinnamon
½ teaspoon ground nutmeg
½ teaspoon salt
3 large bananas (overripe is best)
90 ml/⅓ cup melted coconut oil, plus extra for greasing
60 ml/¼ cup almond milk
1 teaspoon vanilla extract
60 ml/¼ cup maple syrup
80 g/½ cup 70% dark/ bittersweet chocolate chips or roughly chopped chocolate
30 g/¼ cup pecans or walnuts
nut butter or vanilla ice cream, to serve (optional)

12 x 23-cm/9 x 5-inch loaf pan, greased with coconut oil

MAKES 1 LOAF

Preheat the oven to 180°C (350°F) Gas 4.

Mix together the dry ingredients (flours, baking powder, spices and salt) in a medium bowl.

Mash the bananas in another bowl, then add the melted coconut oil, almond milk, vanilla and maple syrup and mix everything together using a rubber spatula.

Gradually mix the dry ingredients into the banana mixture until everything is well combined. Fold in the chocolate chips.

Pour the batter into the prepared loaf pan and sprinkle the top with the pecans or walnuts. Bake the loaf in the preheated oven for 45–50 minutes, rotating halfway through the cooking time.

Remove from the oven and leave to cool to room temperature in the pan before turning out. Serve toasted with nut butter for breakfast, or warm with vanilla ice cream for dessert.

sweet potato chocolate mousse

I was very surprised by these little cups of mousse when I first made them. They were so easy to throw together (just seven ingredients all in one bowl!) and the flavour was just what I was looking for – dark chocolatey and lightly sweetened. This mousse is more true to a dense (yet fluffy) chocolate mousse than other avocado-based versions.

I love portioning them into little jars for a snack or dessert to grab throughout the week – they keep well in the fridge for 5–6 days.

I like to serve them with a little sprinkle of sea salt and coconut whipped cream, if I have it.

1 large sweet potato, scrubbed clean
5 tablespoons good-quality cocoa powder
60 ml/¼ cup maple syrup
3 tablespoons coconut cream
1 tablespoon coconut oil
1 tablespoon ground chia seeds
sprinkle of flaky sea salt, to serve

2 small sterilized jars or glasses (optional)

SERVES 2

Preheat the oven to 200°C (400°F) Gas 6.

Poke the sweet potato with a fork a few times, place on the oven rack, and bake in the preheated oven for 45–60 minutes, or until it's soft when you squeeze it.

Remove from the oven and allow the the sweet potato to cool in the foil. Once cool, peel the skin off (it should come off easily now).

Put the sweet potato flesh into a medium-sized bowl and mash roughly with a fork to break it up.

Mix in the remaining ingredients (apart from the sea salt to serve) using a wooden spoon or a hand-held electric whisk, until smooth. For the fluffiest, best results, I use a hand-held electric whisk.

Portion into small jars or glasses and place in the fridge for at least an hour or overnight. Sprinkle the mousses with flaky sea salt when you are ready to serve.

socca pancakes *with pear & tahini drizzle*

Like a sweet crepe, but with a little more structure, this dessert uses chickpea (gram) flour to make the nutty, protein-rich socca. The pear and maple-tahini topping is also nice served with yogurt, ice cream or waffles. Both the pears and the sauce can be made in advance and the pears can be warmed up before topping the socca.

Socca Pancakes (page 29)

FOR THE PEARS
melted coconut oil, for
   brushing
2 firm pears (such as Bosc)
   sliced lengthwise into
   0.5-cm/¼-inch thick
   slices
¼ teaspoon ground
   cinnamon, plus more
   if needed

**FOR THE MAPLE-TAHINI
DRIZZLE**
60 g/¼ cup tahini
60 ml/¼ cup almond milk
1–2 tablespoons maple
   syrup
¼ teaspoon ground
   cinnamon
¼ teaspoon vanilla extract

*baking tray, lined with
baking parchment*

SERVES 2

Preheat the oven to 180°C (350°F) Gas 4.

Brush the baking parchment on the baking tray with a thin layer of melted coconut oil and arrange the pear slices on top in a single layer. Brush the pears with more melted coconut oil and then sprinkle with cinnamon.

Bake in the preheated oven for 30–40 minutes, flipping them at the 20-minute mark, until the pears have softened and are beginning to turn golden.

Meanwhile, prepare the maple-tahini drizzle. In a small bowl or jar, combine the tahini, almond milk, maple syrup, cinnamon and vanilla. Whisk by hand or use a stick blender to blend together until smooth.

Top the warm socca pancakes with the maple-tahini drizzle and pears and serve.

aquafaba pavlova *with fresh fruit*

Aquafaba is the water that chickpeas are cooked in. This often-discarded ingredient amazingly acts like egg whites in many dishes, making a great plant-based substitution in a pavlova.

You'll notice regular old sugar is used here. While I really wanted to make a pav using maple or honey, you just don't get the same crispy outer shell without a finely ground sugar.

This recipe can actually be a bit of a diva – whipping times can vary, but you're looking for a thickened mixture with soft peaks in the first phase of whipping, and stiff, glossy peaks in the second phase. You should be able to turn the bowl upside down without the mixture moving at the end of whipping.

I've also found that the best aquafaba for this recipe comes from no-added salt (low sodium) organic canned chickpeas and it has to be really well chilled in the fridge.

All of that being said, the prep is actually pretty easy and fast if you have all your ducks in a row.

Your end result should have a crispy outer shell with a slightly hollow, soft, chewy – almost marshmallowy inside. Don't worry if your pavlova gets a little deflated after cooking, you're going to top it with cream and fresh fruit anyway.

150 g/¾ cup caster/
    superfine sugar
2 tablespoons arrowroot
    powder or cornflour/
    cornstarch
pinch of salt
liquid from 1 x 400-g/14-oz.
    can of no-added salt
    (low sodium) organic
    chickpeas, chilled in the
    fridge overnight
1 teaspoon white vinegar
1 teaspoon vanilla extract

TO SERVE
whipped cream or whipped
    coconut cream (page 163)
220 g/1½ cups fresh fruit
    (I like berries, sliced
    peaches or mangoes)
icing/confectioners' sugar
    for dusting (optional)

*large baking tray, lined
with baking parchment*

SERVES 6-8

Preheat the oven to 150°C (300°F) Gas 2.

Place a large mixing bowl in the freezer for a few minutes to make it extra cold. In another bowl, combine the sugar, arrowroot (or cornflour/cornstarch) and salt.

In the large chilled bowl, put the chilled aquafaba liquid (straight out of the fridge) and vinegar and beat with a hand-held electric whisk or in a stand mixer at a medium speed for about 2–4 minutes, until soft peaks begin to form, scraping down the sides of the bowl once or twice.

While still mixing, start adding the sugar mixture, one spoonful at a time. When all the sugar has been added, beat for about 3–6 minutes until stiff, glossy peaks form. Add the vanilla and beat for another 10 seconds.

Tip the mixture onto the prepared baking tray and form into a 20-cm/8-inch wide circle using a rubber spatula. Leave space around the edges, as it will spread a bit.

Put in the oven and immediately lower the heat to 120°C (250°F) Gas ½. Bake for 1½–2 hours until the outer shell is hardened when you tap it. Turn off the heat and allow the pavlova to cool completely inside the closed oven – sometimes I'll make it at night and leave it there until the morning. When ready, top with whipped cream, fruit and icing/confectioners' sugar and serve immediately.

chocolate bark *with coconut and cherries*

Over the years, Fabian and I have developed a totally boring and wonderful nightly routine that consists of big mugs of rooibos tea, dark/bittersweet chocolate and the couch. We'll chat about our days, watch some TV and unwind – it's simple and ends the day on a happy note.

This fruit and nut-style bark gets thrown into the rotation to mix it up every now and then.

25 g/¼ cup chopped pecans

15 g/¼ cup coconut flakes

35 g/¼ cup dried cherries
or raisins

200 g/7 oz. dark/
bittersweet chocolate
(70% cocoa solids or
higher), roughly chopped

1 teaspoon maple syrup

flaked sea salt (such as
Maldon)

*a baking tray, lined with
baking parchment*

MAKES ABOUT 4-6 SERVINGS

Preheat the oven to 180°C (350°F) Gas 4.

Spread the pecans out on a baking tray. Roast in the preheated oven for 5 minutes. Toss the pecans and add the coconut flakes to the tray. Return to the oven for 2–3 minutes until the coconut is golden. Remove from the oven and transfer to a plate to cool.

Once cool, mix together the toasted pecans and coconut with the dried cherries or raisins in a small bowl.

Create a double boiler with a small saucepan filled one third of the way with boiling water. Place a larger heatproof bowl (large enough so that it rests above the level of boiling water but comfortably sits atop the saucepan) on top.

Keeping the water at a simmer over a low heat, place the chocolate in the bowl above the boiling water. Stir with a rubber spatula until the chocolate is completely melted, then remove the bowl from the heat. Stir in the maple syrup followed by half of the nut and dried fruit mixture.

Pour the chocolate mix onto the parchment-lined baking tray. Sprinkle with the remaining pecans, coconut and cherries or raisins and a couple of pinches of sea salt. Press down lightly with a clean rubber spatula so that the topping is firmly set within the chocolate.

Leave to cool. (You can place it in the fridge or freezer to speed this process up, especially if it's particularly warm in the kitchen.) Break apart into pieces and store in a sealed box in the fridge.

index

A

aglio e olio quinoa bowl 82
aquafaba pavlova with
fresh fruit 170
aubergine po'boys, roasted
125
avocados: basic avocado
dip 17
everything avocado toast
41
guacamole 104

B

bananas: banana & seed
toast 34
chocolate banana bread
165
bánh mì bowl 85
beetroot: black bean & beet
burgers 122
berries: berry compote 33
peanut butter & berry
toast 34
black beans: barbecue black
beans 9
black bean & beet
burgers 122
butternut squash & black
bean chilli 62
bowls: aglio e olio quinoa
bowl 82
autumn butternut
squash noodle bowl 98
bánh mì bowl 85
cblt salad bowl 82
coconut brown rice bowl
90
cumin spiced pumpkin
bowl 81
green kitchari bowl 78
mezze bowl 77
niçoise-ish salad bowl 94
plantain bowl 86
soy & ginger delicata
winter squash bowl 97
stir fry bowl 101
sweet potato noodle
bowl 74
winter vegetable bowl 89
bread: cauliflower steak

sandwiches 117
broccoli: broccoli pesto 14
pan-grilled broccoli 22
broth, ginger coconut 56
bruschetta party 150–1
buffalo cauliflower &
chickpea bowl 93
burgers, black bean & beet
122

C

cabbage: 5-seed slaw 22
cakes: chocolate banana
bread 165
carrots: carrot soup 60
roasted carrot &
hummus toast 38
cashews: romesco sauce 14
cauliflower: buffalo
cauliflower & chickpea
bowl 93
cauliflower steak
sandwiches 117
leek, cauliflower & fennel
soup 52
cblt salad bowl 82
chermoula 14
cherries, chocolate bark
with coconut and 173
chai & turmeric porridge 30
chickpea flour: chickpea &
chocolate chip cookies
156
chickpea socca pancakes
29
chickpeas: buffalo
cauliflower & chickpea
bowl 93
chickpea 'tikka' masala 108
crispy chickpeas 9
hummus 144–5
chillies: butternut squash
& black bean chilli 62
creamy chipotle dip 17
chocolate: chickpea &
chocolate chip cookies
156
chocolate banana bread
165
chocolate bark with
coconut and cherries
173
hazelnut chocolate

spread toast 34
sweet potato chocolate
mousse 166
coconut: chocolate bark
with coconut 173
coconut bacon bits 21
coconut Bircher muesli 33
coconut cream peach
parfaits 163
coconut milk: coconut
brown rice bowl 90
ginger coconut broth 56
pumpkin coconut soup 59
compote, berry 33
cookies, chickpea &
chocolate chip 156
courgettes: melted
courgette & leek dip 151
roasted courgettes 119
crisps, oven-baked
rosemary 140
crumble cups, strawberry
159
curry: chickpea 'tikka'
masala 108
red lentil dahl 66
Thai vegetable curry 70

D

dahl, red lentil 66
dips 17, 151
dressings 10–13
dukkah 20
dumplings, sweet potato 137

F

fajita filling, veggie 105
falafels, sweet potato 115
farro risotto with green
peas 134
fennel: butternut & fennel
piadinas 146–7
leek, cauliflower & fennel
soup 52
fig & tahini toast 37
fruit, aquafaba pavlova
with fresh 170

G

garlic: garlic greens 21
garlic yogurt dip 17
ginger: ginger coconut
broth 56

soy & ginger delicata
winter squash bowl 97
granola: maple crunch
granola 163
savoury-sweet granola 20
greens, garlic 21
guacamole 104

H

harissa paste: butternut &
harissa hummus 144
tahini-harissa dressing 13
hazelnut chocolate spread
toast 34
herbs: chermoula 14
herb dressings 10
herby slaw 125
hummus 38, 144–5

J

jerk spice roasted
vegetables 90

K

kale: white bean & kale dip
151
kitchari bowl, green 78

L

leeks: leek, cauliflower &
fennel soup 52
melted courgette & leek
dip 151
lentils: miso lentils 60
Moroccan-spiced lentil
stew 65
mushroom & lentil no
meat-balls 133
red lentil dahl 66

M

maple crunch granola 163
meringues: aquafaba
Pavlova 170
mezze bowl 77
miso paste: miso lentils 60
miso mushroom soup 61
Moroccan-spiced lentil
stew 65
mousse, sweet potato
chocolate 166
muesli, coconut bircher 33
mushrooms: miso

mushroom soup 61
mushroom & lentil no
  meat-balls 133
seared mushrooms 119

N
nachos, vegetable-loaded
  149
niçoise-ish salad bowl 94
noodles: autumn butternut
  squash noodle bowl 98
  ginger coconut broth 56
  sweet potato noodle
    bowl 74

O
oats: chai & turmeric
  porridge 30
  savoury-sweet granola
    20
onions, caramelized 18

P
paella, vegetable 129
pancakes, socca 29, 169
parfaits, coconut cream
  peach 163
pasta, roasted tomato date
  night 112
pavlova, aquafaba 170
peach parfaits, coconut
  cream 163
peanut butter: peanut
  butter & berry toast 34
  peanut dressing 12
pear, socca pancakes with
  169
peas: farro risotto with
  green peas 134
  peas & spinach on toast
    38
pecans, poached apples
  with maple 160
peppers: romesco sauce 14
  stuffed poblano peppers
    111
pesto: baking tray pizza
  with pesto winter
  squash 126
  broccoli pesto 14
piadinas 146–7
pine nuts: za'atar & pine
  nut hummus 145

pizza, baking tray 126
plantain bowl 86
poached apples with maple
  pecans 160
po'boys, roasted aubergine
  125
polenta party 118–19
porridge, chai & turmeric 30
potatoes: niçoise-ish salad
  bowl 94
pumpkin: cumin spiced
  pumpkin bowl 81
  pumpkin coconut soup 59

Q
quinoa: aglio e olio quinoa
  bowl 82

R
ratatouille, roasted
  vegetable 130
rice: bánh mì bowl 85
  coconut brown rice bowl
    90
  green kitchari bowl 78
  stir fry bowl 101
  stuffed poblano peppers
    111
  vegetable paella 129
risotto, farro 134
romesco sauce 14

S
salads: 5-seed slaw 22
  herby slaw 125
salsa, tomato basil 150
sandwiches: cauliflower
  steak sandwiches 117
  vegan breakfast
    sandwich 42
seeds: banana & seed toast
  34
  5-seed slaw 22
smoothie bowl, green 26
socca pancakes 29, 169
soups: carrot soup 60
  creamy roasted tomato
    soup 51
  ginger coconut broth 56
  green Thai soup 55
  leek, cauliflower & fennel
    soup 52
  miso mushroom soup 61

pumpkin coconut soup 59
spring vegetable soup 48
spinach: peas & spinach on
  toast 38
squash: autumn butternut
  squash noodle bowl 98
  baking tray pizza with
    pesto winter squash
    126
  butternut & harissa
    hummus 144
  butternut squash & black
    bean chilli 62
  piadinas with butternut
    & fennel 146–7
  soy & ginger delicata
    winter squash bowl 97
  vegan breakfast
    sandwich 42
stews: Moroccan-spiced
  lentil stew 65
  sweet potato & white
    bean stew 69
stir fry bowl 101
strawberry crumble cups
  159
sweet potatoes: savoury
  brekkie sweet potato
  45
  spicy sweet potato filling
    105
  sweet brekkie sweet
    potato 45
  sweet potato & white
    bean stew 69
  sweet potato chocolate
    mousse 166
  sweet potato dumplings
    137
  sweet potato falafel 115
  sweet potato noodle
    bowl 74
  sweet potato wedges 143

T
taco party 104–5
tahini: dressings 12–13
  fig & tahini toast 37
  socca pancakes with pear
    & tahini drizzle 169
Thai soup, green 55
Thai vegetable curry 70
toasts 34–41

tofu, spicy 10
tomatoes: blistered
  tomatoes 119
  creamy roasted tomato
    soup 51
  roasted tomato date
    night pasta 112
  tomato & white beans
    with toast 39
  tomato basil salsa 150
toppings 18–20
tortilla chips: vegetable-
  loaded nachos 149

V
vegan breakfast sandwich
  42
vegetables: jerk spice
  roasted vegetables 90
  roasted vegetable
    ratatouille 130
  spring vegetable soup 48
  Thai vegetable curry 70
  vegetable-loaded nachos
    149
  vegetable paella 129
  winter vegetable bowl 89
vinaigrette 11

W
walnut 'breadcrumbs' 18
white beans: piadinas
  146–7
  sweet potato & white
    bean stew 69
  tomato & white beans
    with toast 39
  white bean & kale dip 151
  white bean purée 125
winter vegetable bowl 89

Y
yellow split peas: green
  kitchari bowl 78
yogurt: garlic yogurt dip 17

Z
za'atar 81
  za'atar & pine nut
    hummus 145
zucchini *see courgette*

acknowledgments

A big thank you to Cindy Richards for your enthusiasm about this book from the get go. Thank you to Sharon Bowers, for being a rockstar agent and giving me reliably great advice. To Rebecca Ffrench for your help in making me realize my book dream could become a reality.

To my editor Alice Sambrook, for keeping this book in check and for volunteering to make that finicky pav. Thank you to Megan Smith for the beautiful design work. Food stylist Emily Kydd and photographer Clare Winfield for making my recipes look better than I could have imagined.

A huge thank you to Jessica Murnane for sharing your sage cookbook knowledge and all your lovely recipe testers – you guys are seriously amazing and I will be forever grateful for your help.

My wonderful fellow editors at mindbodygreen, you guys inspire me to be smarter and even more curious about the wellness world every day.

To Mom, Gammy, Poppy and the rest of the McSherrys, thank you for always making sure I never went without broccoli or Friday night pizza. So much love to the Vanderveldts, and particularly Dad, for being obsessed with cooking and eating the most delicious things. To the Roches and Smiths, for the memorable themed dinner parties.

Shout out to my pizza witches for trekking out to Brooklyn to eat my food and to Babs for making me laugh throughout the day. You guys are the most loyal and supportive friends I could ask for. And finally, to Fabian, words can't express my gratitude and appreciation for your love and partnership. I'm so lucky that I found you.